What Dr. Deepak's Patients Say About Him

"He was compassionate when I lost my son... He saved my husband's life... He really cared and showed us his kindness."

Molly L.

"Such a fine man and doctor. He spends time with my husband who has Alzheimer's and makes sure he understands his condition."

Tammy S.

"Dr. Deepak was chosen by God to be a Doctor. Always so kind, sweet, and reassuring all will be fine."

Kathryn M.

"He has been a wonderful friend and such a kind and caring doctor... He has been such a blessing to so many people in our area..."

Glynn P.

"He is a super doctor... He is the one that found my husbands cancer... This is to say how caring he is for both of us in watching our hearts."

Joyce M.

"I also was blessed to have him as my doctor for 6 years. Great bedside manner and he cared for all of us, which made me feel so good to have him. He saved my life and I will miss him dearly. Good luck to you and your family, Sir! Zachary will miss you immensely!"

Karen V.

"I was so upset when I found out he was going to retire. I have seen him from the first week he was at the Cardiovascular Institute of the South. I cried and will see him for the last time Tuesday. Prayers for this gentle and wonderful man. He will be greatly missed."

Je G.

"I love him too! My husband and I are patients of his and we really hate to see him retire. But I wish him a life full of adventures for him and his family. Good, good man who we will miss."

Pamela L.

"Dr. Deepak is absolutely awesome! My husband and I both go to him and love him! We are sad to know that he's retiring, but we definitely understand! We never could have asked for or gotten a better doctor! Thank you, Dr. Deepak, for your service to your patients over the years, for your care and concern, and for being such a wonderful doctor. We wish you the absolute best in your retirement years! Again, THANK YOU!!"

Anonymous

"He is my savior. He saved my life in 2010 after three heart attacks. His expertise and treatment added years to my recovery and my life. Thank you, Dr. Deepak, and may God in His infinite wisdom continue to bless and guide you in the years to come. May our heavenly Father bless and keep you in your years ahead in your retirement."

Anonymous

"Dr. Deepak has been our doctor for years—a very kind, humble, smart, intelligent, understanding, caring, friendly, approachable, down-to-earth doctor, which is very rare to find. I run out of positive, good, kind words to describe him; he's like family. All rolled into one, he's an incredible, magnificent person and doctor all rolled into one. God bless him and his family."

Anonymous

Silk and Clay

Deepak Thekkoott, M.D.

ISBN 979-8-9997758-2-5 Hardcover
ISBN 979-8-9997758-3-2 Softcover
ISBN 979-8-9997758-4-9 E-book

Library of Congress Control Number: 2025917042
Printed in the United States of America
First Edition

Book design by Houston Creative Space
Author photograph by Paula Nguyen Luu

Palm Leaf Press
Houston, Texas

palm
leaf
press

Silk and Clay

A Physician's Journey of Cancer, Survival, and Restored Faith

Deepak Thekkoott, M.D.

palm leaf press

To my wife and our son
To patients, past, present, and future
And to all providers dealing with cancer on the front lines

Contents

Foreword

There are moments in life that change everything. Not just the course of a day or a diagnosis, but the trajectory of a soul. I had the extraordinary privilege of bearing witness to such a moment in the life of Dr. Deepak Thekkoott—and to walk beside him through the landscape of trauma, fear, and ultimately, profound transformation.

When Deepak was diagnosed with a rare and aggressive cancer, the news landed like a whisper wrapped in a thunderclap. It was quiet and clinical, and yet it roared through every part of his life. The odds were grim. The treatments were grueling. But what unfolded in the months that followed was nothing short of astonishing—not because the pain and despair weren't real (they were), but because of the man he chose to be in the face of it all.

I watched a physician—someone trained to fix, to cure, to remain composed—become a patient brought to his knees. But in that collapse, I saw something far greater than strength. I saw courage—not just to survive, but to feel everything. I saw kindness—not just for others, but slowly, and with effort, for himself. And I saw fortitude—not loud or defiant, but quiet, sacred, and enduring.

There were days when the weight of the unknown was unbearable. Times when fear crept in like smoke, suffocating sleep, peace, and even hope. I was there when the dreams turned dark, when the body failed, when the faith trembled. But I was also there when he began to rise—not with certainty, but with humility. Not with answers, but with trust.

Silk and Clay is not just a story of illness. It is a testimony to what it means to live with soul-deep honesty. To let your body be reshaped by suffering and your spirit softened by grace. To be clay—broken, fired, and formed anew. And to be silk—resilient, fluid, luminous with the light of faith.

This book is deeply personal to me because I didn't just hear about Deepak's journey—I was part of it. I walked beside him, sometimes in silence, sometimes in tears, sometimes holding the thread of hope when he couldn't. I saw him find meaning in the middle of the storm, and I saw him offer that meaning back to the world.

If you are facing your own crisis, or walking with someone through theirs, may this story be your companion. It is honest. It is raw. But it is also deeply human, deeply spiritual, and deeply hopeful.

This is not the end of Deepak's story. It is a beginning—a tender, hard-won invitation to all of us: to live fully, to love more deeply, and to believe, even in the dark, that healing is possible.

Dr. Mike Klaybor, Ph.D.
Psychotherapist
Houston, Texas

"Do not worry. You have always written before and you will write now. All you have to do is write one true sentence. Write the truest sentence you know."

—Ernest Hemingway, *A Moveable Feast*

The Last Patient of the Day

Day 1: Zachary, Louisiana, February 26, 2018

Out of nowhere, a cramp in my right leg.

Mondays were my "vein days." My last patient of the day was an elderly woman I had known for years. At this point in my career, I could perform sclerotherapy—injecting a solution into an affected vein, irritating it enough that it swells shut—with my eyes closed. So much of what cardiologists do is preventative, nudging the body to redirect, divert, and adjust to blockages or potential occlusion.

After years practicing in rural India, London, and Brooklyn, I had been working in Zachary, a bedroom community near Baton Rouge, for the past nine years.

Zachary would be a mere drop of blood, if observed at all, on most maps. But like that red globule, it contained a universe of home, work, and friends. And like all places, it was teeming with history. During the Civil War, the battle for nearby Port Hudson had gone unstaunched for months. With their victory, the Union fully reclaimed the Mississippi. Industrial plants now line the riverbanks near Zachary, including a large paper mill and the largest petroleum refinery in the country. This section of the Mississippi River corridor is also known as "Cancer Alley."

Most days, I left home around 6:30 in the morning and reached my office shortly before 7:00. As in our own body arteries, the main thoroughfares usually conveyed a lot of traffic and, sometimes, congestion.

After Hurricane Katrina devastated New Orleans in 2005, many families moved west to Baton Rouge, quickly doubling its population. Many of my patients hail from New Orleans and miss it. A transplant several times over myself, I can relate. I can also especially understand a lifetime longing for New Orleans, a city like none else. Despite its rough and tumble nature, the soul of Crescent City is one of overwhelming freedom expressed through music and a love of food. Like the Mississippi crisscrossing the city, the never-ending LOVE flows through its arteries and veins.

It was in Louisiana where I blossomed into a loving, caring physician. My patients appreciated me and my approach to medicine. I felt cherished from my first moment there and held through the most difficult challenge of my life.

❀

The nurses had already prepped my patient's right leg. I began the routine procedure, something I've done to others causing them as little discomfort as humanly possible, hundreds of times over the years and the second time for this particular patient.

Instead, something started within me.

At first, I thought nothing of the stabbing pain in my own right leg and waited for it to pass, mentally waving it away as an especially horrible muscle cramp. Perhaps I hadn't stretched my leg well enough after my most recent CrossFit training session.

But every time I tried to begin, the feeling intensified, becoming more intolerable, not less.

Apologizing to my patient, I assured her I would be back in a few minutes. As calmly as I could on trembling legs, I left the room and entered my office, around the corner from the procedure room.

Once inside, I planted my hands on the wall in a kind of upright push-up position, hoping that stretching my calf and hamstring would ease the tightness out and return them to normal functioning without the brain-searing pain. But a moment later, I crumpled to the floor.

My staff trickled in. The nurses thought this was a muscle spasm, too, and kneeled next to me to help stretch my leg.

I started to sweat and my mouth dried to chalk.

A few minutes later, my colleague, Dr. Charles Thompson—Chuck—entered. He was seeing patients next door, and the nurses had called him when they saw me leave the procedure room looking unwell. Prior to becoming a cardiologist, he had spent years as an emergency medical technician. After a few questions and a quick exam, he was certain that I had a slipped disc and told me I needed to go to the ER immediately.

By now, I was lying helplessly on the floor, in desperate need of relief. The overwhelming torment felt like it was coming from deep within my bones.

Now that I'm on the other side of it, I can come nearer to appreciating the pain. The procedure that it interrupted, sclerotherapy, might sound counterintuitive, but when the blood vessel slams shut, the healing process can begin. The closure allows the body to reabsorb the blocked vein, and blood reroutes, sluicing through to more open channels. I view my journey, beginning that routine moment in my office, in much the same way: an unfathomable block that ultimately forged deeper, more expansive ways of being.

Down the Dim Corridor

July 6, 2020: MD Anderson, Houston, TX

A hot, humid, stuporous summer day.

My wife, Deepa, our son, Soorya, and I had once again journeyed from our home to the Rotary House Hotel on Holcombe Boulevard, Houston, Soorya doing most of the driving.

This hotel had become our home away from home. The chandelier-lit lobby with its large coffee station at one end, a mini library tucked beside it. An elegant restaurant on the second floor offering freshly cooked meals and a wooden bar gleaming with polish stocked with scotches and good wines. The epitome of grace and courtesy. An essential reminder of life, which needs to go on as long as we are here to live it.

Despite this graciousness on the part of the hotel and its kind staff, no guest wanted or wished to be there. We were immensely grateful for the building, the compassionate staff, and the carefully chosen amenities, but we were only staying here because we had no other choice. All of us at the ends of the proverbial line of trains that we desperately wanted to slow, stop, or reroute completely.

❀

I woke up early that morning, the air still mostly dark. As usual, I had struggled to get a good night's sleep. The same was true for my loving wife. She immersed herself in prayer a few days before and after each visit here, but even her deep faith couldn't completely quell her worry.

Slipping quietly out of the room, careful not to wake Deepa or Soorya, I trod softly down the corridor. It was always too quiet, the lights eerily dim. The elevator thumped down several floors and sighed into the empty lobby.

I made my way to the main doors and pushed them open with some effort—condensed water vapor from the already humid day had created a kind of seal. As I stepped outside, the blunt, too-warm morning air formed a nearly palpable wall.

Desperate for somewhere I could watch everyday life unfold around me, I beelined to a quiet garden on the property and sat gratefully on a bench. I needed to prepare myself to take on the challenges I would soon face: the rush of meetings, and yes, procedures. But this time and for the past more than two years, only procedures that were done to me, for my own good.

In a few hours it would all begin. Again.

Blast Crisis

Day 1: Zachary, Louisiana, February 26, 2018

The emergency room is next door to the clinic, but my office manager insisted on driving me to the hospital. A wheelchair was brought to transport me to a corner room, number 21, familiar to me from my many visits to my patients who'd landed here. It was the only empty bed in the ER that afternoon and faced the nursing station, giving the nurses and doctors a clear view of my condition. This particular room is usually reserved for patients needing close observation, like those on suicide watch.

In truth, all the rooms in the ER are familiar to me. As a cardiologist, I have seen hundreds of patients in these rooms over the years, before now always from the other side of danger. The calming expert rather than the panicked patient.

Soon after I checked in, Chuck joined me to keep me company. He had finished the procedure on my patient.

Dr. Brent Giuffre was the attending ER physician that afternoon. I was happy to see him. All ER attendings were my friends as we worked closely together. Brent, too, suspected a slipped disc, but wanted to confirm it. He examined me and gave me multiple intravenous pain medications. He ordered X-rays, a CT scan, and complete blood work. The pain medications didn't seem to be effective. All they did was give me an incredibly dry mouth.

Brent came by with a perplexed look around fifteen minutes after completing my tests. Looking into his eyes, I could see that something was not right. He told me that my CT scans were normal, but my blood work was not. In fact, it was very abnormal. My white blood cell count was 87,000. The normal white cell count is anywhere between 4,000 and 11,000. While I am not a cancer expert, I could recognize how scary this was—a very high white blood cell count is a sign of cancer. Brent also informed me that 13% blast cells were present. Blast cells are immature cells that are produced by and emitted from the bone marrow when it activates an overdrive production mode. Typically, blast cells are not present in the cell count at all.

Brent wanted to redo my blood work. "Deepak, this could be a mistake," he said, but the lines in his brow remained deeply grooved.

Something in me told me that my blood work would not come back any different.

In less than five minutes, Brent was back with my second blood test results. I could see the sadness in his expression as he rushed into my room. The results were unchanged. He gave me the second report.

As I examined the lab report, I immediately knew it was leukemia. Specifically, it looked like AML, Acute myeloid leukemia. A type of blood cancer that affects the bone marrow and blood, the most common leukemia in adults. This explained my pain. It was caused by the rapid and uncontrolled multiplication of bone marrow cells inside my leg bone, the tibia. In medical terms, this is called a blast crisis. For me, it was the foremost crisis of my life. I understood that my life was in imminent danger.

At that moment, though, all I could think about was my wife, Deepa. *How am I going to tell her this news? How is she going to take it? How is Soorya, my son, going to handle this news? What will happen to our family? Who is going to take care of them?*

Strangely, I was not scared. I didn't feel any sadness. Other than my fears for my wife and son, I was calm. My whole life passed through my mind, painted on one long canvas gently pulled across my field of vision.

This effect is the most distinct memory I have of that moment. The sudden awareness of my mortality numbed me.

I clearly needed more specialized care than what I could find at our small, local hospital. I called my friend, Dr. Mike Castine. He's an outstanding hematologist who had been a cancer doctor for many years with a large practice in Zachary. I'd referred many of my patients to him. He took my call, and I explained the situation. He also spoke to Brent and immediately arranged for my transfer to the Baton Rouge General Medical Center cancer unit, where he was also on staff. He recommended that I start Hydroxyurea, which works by actively reducing the white blood cell count. It usually takes three to five days to bring the white cell count down to normal levels. Bringing my white blood cell count down immediately was critical. These high counts could cause kidney damage and potentially plug up my arteries. It could also lead to significant breathing difficulties, affecting the blood flow to the lungs.

As I was about to board the ambulance that would carry me to Baton Rouge, Chuck took my right hand and raised it. He prayed for me, asking that my doctors and nurses would be filled with wisdom as they treated me. He prayed to God for my healing and asked Jesus to intervene on my behalf.

Tears streamed from my eyes. This was one of the most beautiful and kindest acts I have ever received in my life. At that moment, he transformed from a medical healer into a spiritual one, asking higher powers to intervene on my behalf and deliver miracles. Even now, I cannot think of that moment without experiencing a rush of emotions.

Soon, the ambulance would carry me along the same route I traveled daily in my commute to work.

❀

I was boarded onto a gurney and slowly transferred to the ambulance. A crowd had already formed. Cheryl, whom I knew as a nurse for a long time, had cared for me in the ER. She hugged me as I was leaving. Brent said good luck. My partners, nurses, Cath lab workers, and office staff all watched silently, in disbelief at the sudden turn of events.

I waved goodbye and started my journey to the unknown.

❋

Although we were more than content in Zachary, ever since Soorya went off to college, Deepa and I had been on the lookout for our next destination.

We were travelers by nature: Europe, the Middle East, Africa, and South America. We spent our twenty-fifth wedding anniversary in the Easter Islands among the Moai statues. At the time of my cancer diagnosis, we had been looking forward to our next family trip to Machu Picchu and the Galápagos Islands. We were set to leave in just two weeks with Soorya. Now, amidst the storm of this uncertain diagnosis, the ancient sanctuary and the even more ancient turtles would have to wait.

❋

It takes around thirty minutes to reach Baton Rouge General. The ambulance sped along the interstate, past my home. They took me to the cancer floor. My room was ready, and the nurses were waiting. It was a single room, spacious enough. The curtains were open.

The room had a large window. It was already dark.

❋

I had not called Deepa yet. I didn't know what to tell her. I was also still in a great deal of pain. Fortunately, Chuck's wife, Donna, and Deepa have been close friends for years. Donna had been a respiratory therapist, but she had stopped working to stay home with her children. At the time, Donna was mourning the recent loss of her mother. As soon as Mike arranged for me to be transferred to the cancer unit at Baton Rouge General Medical Center, Chuck called Donna, who then called Deepa. Donna told my wife that I had some back and leg pain issues and that I needed specialty care. She also told her that I was being transferred to the hospital in Baton Rouge. Donna arranged to pick Deepa up and take her to the hospital.

Chuck called Deepa. He repeated the same narrative that I had some issues with severe muscle spasms in my back and leg and needed treatment in Baton Rouge. Both he and Donna felt that they should not be the ones to deliver such news as a cancer diagnosis.

Later, Chuck and Donna told me Deepa kept asking, "Is he going to be okay?" They said it was heartbreaking.

I was anything but okay. I was still in agonizing pain. At the oncology ward of the Baton Rouge General Medical Center, they gave me Morphine, Dilaudid, and Demerol, all highly potent pain meds. They also gave me Toradol, an anti-inflammatory medicine, and applied a Fentanyl patch. The medicines made me incredibly drowsy, and I kept dozing off. I had IV fluids running, and as Mike had suggested, they started Hydroxyurea intravenously.

It wasn't long before I was the star attraction on the floor. A minor crowd quickly built up around my door. Office managers, Cath lab directors, nurse practitioners, and attending colleagues from both my practice in Zachary and our sister practice in Baton Rouge were all there.

Soon, Deepa arrived with Donna. Waiting for her arrival, I knew it would be hard to face her. Donna stayed back, allowing husband and wife this moment. Deepa rushed in and sat on the bed, her face stricken and suddenly old. "Deepak, why are all these people here?"

I looked into her eyes and held her hand, but I couldn't speak. I froze except for the tears pouring down my face. I couldn't tell her my diagnosis. I lay in bed and looked out the windows, away from her and the crowd.

I continued to doze on and off. I had received enough medicine by then that could put a large animal to sleep.

When I next awoke, the crowd had departed. The curtains were still open, revealing the night's black depths. The floor was silent—no noise, no distraction, just the murmur of my IV pump. I looked at my dear wife in sorrow. "Deepa . . . they think I have leukemia." I didn't mention that I had correctly diagnosed myself as well, wanting to hold the dreaded term as far away from me, from my darling wife, as possible, like a radioactive container.

For a nonmedical person, "leukemia" means a miserable and hopeless diagnosis and a fast-arriving death. As calmly as I could, I said. "It's a bad one, but we can fight it."

Without a word, she lay beside me on my hospital bed, and I held her tightly as she shook, sobbing quietly. After several minutes, she gathered herself and started comforting me. She held me tightly as she spoke. She started praying when she ran out of words of assurance for me, her way out of difficult situations in life.

With each passing minute, she seemed to grow stronger. She shook off her sadness and spoke to herself, convincing herself that none of this was true. She kept repeating that everything would be fine. She believed that this was all a mistake.

Trying to make her accept the truth, I told her about the long road ahead. I explained that this journey could last for months and that we needed to inform our son, Soorya.

She could not hear this, instead repeating: "There is nothing wrong with you." She did not believe the blood work. "You're going to be okay," she insisted. "Let's wait for the results of more tests. It's all going to be fine."

For so many years, I was the force she both relied on and cared for. We had been through many ups and downs, and we had crossed oceans together. Even when I made poor choices in my life and career, she stood by me, steered me toward the right path, and never gave up hope for better days ahead. She saw something in me and was willing to give me a second chance when I faltered. However, she was not ready to see me sick and weak, desperately bargaining to live.

Mike Castine, my hematologist, came by around seven in the evening. He sat down beside us. This was the first time I had seen him since we'd spoken over the phone. Deepa had never met him, and she was silent beyond the initial pleasantries of introductions. Sitting next to me, I could feel her whole body fibrillating. Mike explained that he had reviewed the results of my blood work and that I needed a bone marrow aspiration and biopsy as soon as possible. This is a confirmatory test to make a precise diagnosis and help doctors understand my leukemia's exact nature. He explained the procedure to Deepa: drilling deep into the back of the hip to collect a small sample of bone and marrow to be sent to the lab for testing and further analysis. He had arranged for a biopsy that very evening.

Deepa didn't ask any questions, and neither did I.

A nurse wheeled me into a procedure room for the biopsy, Deepa almost trotting alongside to keep up. The results would be available the following day.

Once I was back in my room, Deepa called our only child, our darling. Though he could take care of himself and us, we nevertheless fervently wished to protect Soorya from news that would worry him.

Deepa and I are both close to our son, though she shares an even tighter bond born of frequent international moves and transitions. Even as a three-year-old, Soorya carried himself well when he and Deepa moved from India to join me in England, and adjusted easily to life in the U.S. when we moved again when he was nine. The move from a quiet Welsh elementary school to the inner-city schools of New York was likely difficult, but he adapted quickly. Our son grew up fast and learned to defend himself.

Beginning when he was around ten, he told us he was interested in joining the armed forces. He was fascinated by historical wars and romanticized the idea of being a soldier. He visited West Point in middle school, but had so far refrained from joining the United States Armed Forces, due to the anxiety that appeared on his mother's face whenever he brought it up.

During his college years, Soorya stayed in a dorm in Midtown Manhattan and spent hours wandering around the city. He found solace in public libraries and spent weekends exploring the varied, beautiful public gardens of New York. After watching his first Broadway production, he was hooked, and began reviewing shows for his high school and college student newspapers. A voracious reader and a wonderful writer, he was initially a literature and creative writing major, but changed to medicine in his junior year. His maternal great-grandfather, maternal grandfather, and father were all physicians. Though slightly surprised by this abrupt change, I was happy with his decision. His grandfather was ecstatic.

After college, Soorya joined us in Louisiana and found work in the emergency room at the hospital where I worked. He loved the experience. Working as a technician in the ER reinforced his desire to pursue medicine. He quickly made many friends in the hospital and was the in-house comedian, as well as frequently baking treats for the ER staff. No job was too trivial for him; on many occasions, I saw him mopping the emergency room floor or wiping down the bedside commodes. He beamed when he saw me taking care of patients in the emergency room.

Despite his enthusiasm, Soorya had a hard time getting into a medical school in the United States. He managed to find an international school in the Caribbean willing to accept him. It was based in Saint Lucia and he left the United States for the Caribbean in the fall of 2016. He quickly fell in love with the islands and their culture, made many friends, and loved his studies. We missed him dearly while he was away, but visited him there and had a wonderful time with him and his friends.

Now I could hear him comforting his mother over the phone. He was likely speaking softly and the speakerphone volume was low. "Mom, it's going to be okay. Even in the worst-case scenario, we can give him the best care possible."

"Yes, yes," Deepa was whispering, as if she raised her voice one decibel the walls of our world would tumble down.

Deepa is the most positive person I have ever known; she has long been my strength. She will fight for women's rights as if her life depends upon it. An avid reader, she earned a master's degree in English literature, with a focus on British and American classics. She loves Shakespeare and the Scottish poet Robert Burns. We visited Stratford-upon-Avon and Shakespeare's memorial in Poets' Corner in Westminster Abbey, as well as Robert Burns's birthplace in the village in Ayrshire, Scotland. She loves Robert Frost's poetry and can recite "The Road Not Taken" by heart. There isn't a classic she has yet to read and discuss with our child. Dante's Divine Comedy was her gift to him on his fifteenth birthday.

Deepa loves children and is happiest among them. She worked as a primary school teacher and worked as a substitute in the New York City Public school system in Brooklyn when we lived there. These kids came from all different backgrounds and nationalities with a high percentage of English Language Learners. There were many poor children, and schools were a welcome respite for them. Teachers fed them and gave them stability and comfort. She did all she could to support them, including helping financially with class trips and excursions. During the holidays, we were busy buying toys for her students. In the summer of 2009, she traveled to Tanzania with Soorya to teach in a village near Arusha for six weeks.

When Deepa told Soorya, he said: "Dad has taken care of us over the years. Now, it's our turn to take care of him as best we can."

Silk and Clay

A Watery Sonata

July 6, 2020: MD Anderson, Houston, TX

Morning clouds hovered over the Houston sky, gathered lazily into a heavy, unwanted blanket. A few cars and city buses drove past at this early hour, but the rest of the city hadn't yet revved its engine. Above my head, a proliferation of birds perched on a wire argued with each other. They stared at me and then flew away—I had disturbed their morning routine. They wanted to watch and eavesdrop. But to care about humans? Maybe not so much.

Two early-shift nurses passed by, speaking loudly in Tagalog, which I had become familiar with while working in hospitals in London and New York City, as well as vacationing in the Philippines. I met more Malayalee nurses here than anywhere in the world. They come from Kerala, the southernmost state of India, and their presence was comforting because I am also from Kerala. The spirit of healing is in their blood and shows in their bedside manners.

The fountain across the road played its watery sonata to an empty audience.

From my bench, the skywalk connecting the hotel to another even larger building was starkly visible.

The other building was a hospital. Not any hospital, but MD Anderson, one of the largest and best cancer hospitals in the country, if not the world.

❀

People come from all over the globe for treatment at MD Anderson, the Mecca of cancer care. Like all things in Texas, the building stands big and tall, its ambitions reaching for the moon and the stars. Nobel laureates unassumingly walk the halls.

With an operating budget of nearly $5 billion a year, 700 inpatient beds, and 20,000 staff, breakthroughs in cancer research and treatment occur at Anderson at an inspiring rate. Named for Munro Dunaway Anderson. Anderson made his immense fortune by exploiting Black sharecroppers. And yet, his large donation, matched with the Texas legislature in 1954, created a place of healing and hope.

Some perish here. Some thought to be incurable are cured here. For many, it is the last hope in a fight to stay alive, with its daily miracles, its compassion, and its hope writ large.

The enormity of the hospital—the length and breadth of its atriums and its long verandas—can be overwhelming for first-time visitors, especially patients in pain and full of reasonable fear. Sometimes I couldn't help feeling like a number, a statistic. But that was only on my lowest days. The staff did everything in their power to keep me out of abysses of despair, to insist on my personhood, my aliveness. My continuity.

The staff hails from the U.S. and Canada, South America, the Middle East, Europe, and the rest of Asia. The diversity of staff is a blessing for all patients, especially overseas patients, who take comfort in having a healthcare provider who can speak their native language.

Front office personnel addressed patients on a first-name basis. Each of the hundreds of times I came through, the laboratory staff and the women who scheduled our appointments greeted me warmly. The nurses were so compassionate that their fear for us showed on their faces. They whispered words of encouragement and scolded us when we went off track. I have always had a deep admiration for nursing as a profession. They carry the weight of the world, and it's all in a day's work for them. True angels and nothing less.

Over two years in this hospital and its adjoining hotel, I had spent months at a time as a sickly patient, recovered enough to walk the fluorescent corridors akin to the Valley of the Shadow of Death. I nearly perished there, and at times the suffering was so severe that I wished and prayed that the suffering would end, and I was at peace with any outcome.

The Voice Inside Us

Day 2: Zachary, Louisiana, February 27, 2018

The next day broke and I seemed to feel every crack in my drilled bone. My pain was still horrible, but an iota lessened through the lack of surprise. When I gritted my teeth through a particularly harsh wave, a voice inside me said, "You have leukemia. That's why you are in pain." Even if the answer is unwanted, terrifying, we humans feel comforted by knowledge and patterns. Buried in them, the solution, however faint, glimmers.

More people came to see me.

Ben Boudreaux, who had been my office manager in Zachary for years, stayed by my side in the hospital that day. A few years older than Soorya when he started, he had recently been promoted to vice president of our organization.

Donna and Chuck also came by, along with many of our friends from Zachary and Baton Rouge. They all offered encouraging words. They wanted me to fight. The news spread like wildfire. It was inevitable; I practiced in a small town where everyone knew each other. Prayer chains were already being formed all around Zachary and Baton Rouge.

David Konur, the CEO of our organization, called multiple times. Over our years working together, we had become close, frequently traveling together for both business and pleasure. David and his family had even once spent the holidays with us in New York.

My pain was slowly getting better, though I still experienced intermittent spasms deep in my leg. I was still receiving IV fluids and Hydroxyurea.

Threaded through all of these lovely visits, the waiting. The biopsy results that would guide my treatment plan, a kind of tarnished lantern.

Mike came by in the afternoon. He was visibly upset and avoided making eye contact as he entered my room and sat down on the sofa by the bed. He clutched my biopsy results. Deepa sank next to me on the bed.

He said, "Deepak, it's AML, as we suspected. It looks aggressive."

I had a large number of blast cells in my bone marrow. Some parts of the biopsy results were still pending, such as the molecular typing that would further classify the leukemia. Still, they knew enough to start assembling my treatment plan. Mike also told me that despite modern therapies, AML was an awful cancer and carried a very high mortality rate.

As bad as the news was, I appreciated his honesty as a colleague, a friend, and now, a patient.

He recommended I transfer to MD Anderson Cancer Center in Houston for treatment. "They are best suited for treating leukemias. You will also probably need a bone marrow transplant." Mike stopped talking, his eyes squinting with worry, matching Deepa's and perhaps my own. "Are you okay with me arranging for a transfer?"

I had cared for many patients treated at MD Anderson for different cancers. It is a bona fide center of excellence. I also needed prolonged chemotherapy, which MD Anderson could better handle.

Deepa's hands clutching mine in a tight grip, grim determination on her face. She opened her mouth, but no words came out. I was in shock, suspended in a state of total lack of control over my destiny. It was too much pain and bad news for anyone to handle in a short period of time. I wasn't processing in a logical manner, but I was able to eke out: "Mike, I am going with what you say." I swallowed. "Please proceed."

I felt like a wooden log being carried away in turbulent waters and out to sea. I faced a long road to recovery . . . assuming, of course, that I survived long enough to travel that nightmarish path.

Deepa asked, "Is there any hope?"

"Yes, there is." Mike nodded once, definite. "Let's hope so."

Bone Marrow Biopsy

July 6, 2020: MD Anderson, Houston, TX

I was scheduled for a multitude of tests, including a bone marrow biopsy. My twelfth in two years. My hip bones were scarred where nurses and physician assistants had drilled for marrow. The pain from these invasive and necessary techniques began with a burning like a fire when the local anesthetic—lidocaine—was injected, and blazed into a deep, profound and teeth-clenching ache as they drilled into my skeleton.

The next stage was to aspirate my marrow—literally suck it out, a process that is hard to describe in words. Pain shot from my hip along the length of my leg to my toes. Depending on the day and the person performing the procedure, I—like everyone undergoing this necessary torture—experience a spectrum of pain that one braces against. Yet, it still manages to surprise us with its intensity.

The nurses and Physician's Assistants were skillful and did their best to make me comfortable by explaining each step as they performed the biopsy. Nevertheless, when one is on the receiving end, no amount of smooth talking is enough of a salve for the almost embarrassing amount of discomfort and pain.

After all of that, one tries not to hobble out, a fake smile plastered to our thin faces, overdrawn like a clown's.

From my vantage point on the bench, I watched as Houston slowly warmed up to its usual city activity. People going to work, taking children to school, visiting friends, attacking their to-do's and errands. I had lost these routines—the normal rhythms of work, family life, and social engagements—and I missed them deeply.

I sat facing the trees with my eyes closed. My sickness and the brushes with mortality had changed me, bringing me closer to the higher powers I desperately hoped existed, both beyond human understanding and far from our willingness to accept.

My soul transported me to Mount Kailash in the Himalayas, the abode of Lord Shiva. My forefathers wavered at a distance and my grandmother put her arms around me. She kissed my head and sang her favorite verses from the Bhagavad Gita. Even after they waved goodbye and disappeared, their presence left me with a warm glow in my heart that continued to spread outward, like pond ripples. Humbled, ensorcelled, love from backwards and forwards in time wrapped around me, I asked Lord Shiva to keep me alive.

After the blood work and the bone marrow biopsy, I met with my team of doctors. My transplant doctor, whom we always looked forward to seeing, was on vacation with her school-aged children. She made our visits enjoyable, given the circumstances. She believed that hugging, holding hands, or sitting by a patient's bedside conveyed an understanding of their suffering and a connection to their soul. The very essence of healing.

In her place was a world-renowned expert in post-bone marrow transplant care and in the field of Graft Versus Host Disease (GVHD). He was matter-of-fact, with no time for pleasantries or catching up, but he was also extremely astute and detail-oriented, offering strict instructions for care and recovery. He set the sails for a smooth passage through choppy waters, and I sought to honor his hard work and attentiveness. After him, I saw a skin specialist who was watching me closely for any problems related to transplants and GVHD.

The aim is to keep one alive in the best shape possible.

In the cancer world, this part of my journey is called survivorship: living with cancer from the pain to the diagnosis, through the long days of treatment, until the cancer is in remission.

This wasn't the first time I was enmeshed in the medical world as a patient. When we were ten, my twin and I started experiencing hip pain so severe we began limping. My father took us to an orthopedic surgeon in Thrissur, the district hospital, where the culprit, Legg-Calve-Perthes disease, which affected hip joints in pre-teens, was diagnosed through an X-ray. CT scans and MRIs were not available at the time. My twin's X-rays showed more severe damage compared to mine.

The treatment involved resting the hip joint, which essentially meant using crutches and a leg brace, coupled with frequent X-rays and visits to a professor at Calicut Medical College. The trips to the medical college are vividly sketched in my memory. We traveled on a limited-stop Fast Passenger bus operated by the Kerala State Road Transport Corporation (KSRTC), identifiable by its distinct yellow stripes against a dark green background. The journey took three hours to traverse the mid-Kerala landscape.

During this part of my upbringing, which was acutely challenging and scary, it is notable that my father took over. My mother had a more significant role in my childhood overall, which is common in Indian families. My father, a strict disciplinarian, was often busy with community affairs. I never doubted that he loved us, but my mother managed our day-to-day care.

By seven in the morning, we would be at the bus stop. My father made sure that the driver saw him as he stood on the side of the road and held his hand out, a common posture to hail buses in Kerala. The bus traversed the Kuttippuram Bridge, spanning the largest river in Kerala, the Nila River, a striking sight. The bus stopped in Kuttipuram, where all the passengers and the crew had tea and snacks, and continued to Calicut. From there, we would take a rickshaw to the doctor's house, which was usually crowded with patients. We stayed in a local hotel overnight and returned home the next day. This routine went on for nearly a year and a half.

❋

I was also tested twice afterwards in very unsettling ways. Both times, while traveling abroad, were nerve-wracking experiences. My heart raced and stopped unpredictably, both as a teenager and as an adult. It was infrequent and never lasted very long, so it didn't much concern me, but Deepa was aware of this "tachycardia."

It went away, until one night it woke me up in a hotel in Venice, Italy, around 2 a.m. on our twenty-fifth wedding anniversary. This time, the tachycardia wouldn't stop, giving me the chance to experience Italian healthcare firsthand in the middle of the night. Soon I was carried on a wooden stretcher with a cloth bottom, to which I sank, onto an ambulance moored 500 yards away due to low tide. The half-hour boat ride under a half-moon and a cool ocean breeze hitting my face took me through the canals of Venice. Deepa was next to me, and the crew spoke no English. The same was true for the doctors and nurses at the small hospital where the boat docked. My heart kept racing, and I began to experience chest discomfort. The Italian doctor administered adenosine at my insistence to restore my heart's rhythm. The relief was instant, just as I have seen hundreds of times in my patients. We were back in the hotel before sunrise.

This was the first time I had documented my tachycardia. I self-diagnosed a condition called WPW (Wolff-Parkinson-White) syndrome. The tachycardia could recur, and my Harvard-trained friend Rick Abben recommended an ablation. Within a month, I underwent the procedure with Rick and thought nothing of it afterwards.

November 2017, this time in Marrakech, Morocco. I was travelling with friends, my band of brothers from medical school. The same feeling woke me up at three a.m. My poor heart was racing. Luckily, the taxi arrived at the hotel entrance this time. The international hospital in Marrakesh was poorly equipped. It lacked the necessary medicines. The young, muscular Egyptian doctor—who assumed he knew better than I—and spoke little or no English, gave me a lecture on arrhythmia and what he had on the shelf. A medication called amiodarone. I was not happy. Fortunately, it worked within an hour. I took the next flight home to Louisiana, cutting the trip short. Rick performed a second ablation in late 2017.

While the relationship between my childhood disease, the tachycardias that occurred while I was traveling abroad, and my cancer diagnosis is unclear, I had some practice dealing with pain discomfort and surprises, an alteration of my known world. I could draw on the resources from that experience as I underwent something far more frightening.

Warm Blankets

Day 3: Zachary, Louisiana, February 28, 2018

Up early after a fitful night, I would be transferred in a few hours from Baton Rouge to Houston. David Konur planned to meet me in Houston. As a kind gesture, he had arranged for me to be transported to Houston in an air ambulance.

The plan was to leave in the morning as soon as we had a good weather window. It had been unusually cold and windy in the wee hours, and it needed to be calmer and clearer for our departure.

Mike had already arranged for my transfer to MD Anderson. All the paperwork went through without a problem. This was an important step, as the hospital needed to approve the transfer for insurance purposes. Cancer treatment is an extremely expensive business in the United States, sometimes amounting to millions of dollars for a single patient.

Deepa had already left for Houston early in the morning. Ben volunteered to drive her the whole way to Anderson. I was relieved that she would have company—I was worried about her driving four or five hours to Texas all by herself in her distressed frame of mind. They were on the road by daybreak.

I have no recollection of Deepa leaving the hospital in the morning. When I asked her later, she couldn't remember either. She has no recollection of how she reached Houston except that she went there with Ben and that he drove the entire way. Trauma does that—it swallows memory.

The night before, Deepa had left me in the hospital and went home to pack for an uncertain trip. When she left, she was weak with fear of the unknown. I had never seen her like that before. The whole time she was with me, she cried and prayed. She had never been a worrier until now.

❊

As I waited for my flight to Houston, Donna stopped by my room, hoping to see Deepa. As soon as I updated her on Deepa's state, Donna said, "I'm going to Houston, too then. I need to be with my friend."

We were surrounded by angels. They held us aloft.

❊

We were cleared for take-off just after eight in the morning. I asked for Zofran. I knew that my two-hour helicopter ride to Houston would likely cause nausea, and I didn't want to feel worse than I already did.

For the ride, I was strapped to a very narrow gurney. There was a ramp and a bit of a distance to the helipad. I felt the cold morning air on my cheeks as they rolled me in and lifted the gurney into the helicopter. I lay there in the cramped quarters with my eyes closed. All I could think about were the trips my patients had made over the years in a similar chopper when I had sent them to Houston, Baton Rouge, or New Orleans for emergency surgeries.

I was in good hands here, and I knew it. The pilot and the crew came and introduced themselves. The pilot was a trained U.S. Navy veteran, which gave me comfort. The EMT who would be taking care of me turned out to be a Cath lab technician who knew many of my friends.

The weather remained clear all the way to Houston. We made a pit stop in Lake Charles to refuel. There, they allowed me to stand and walk into the hangar. Soon, we took off for the next leg. I slept mostly during the flight. I was exhausted by now and couldn't wait to land and rest in a proper bed. In Houston, the weather took a turn for the worse, and we were denied permission to land near the hospital. Instead, we had to land the chopper at Hobby Airport near MD Anderson. It was approaching noon by the time we landed.

Once we were on the ground, I thanked the air ambulance crew. From the airport, an ambulance took me through the streets of Houston to MD Anderson. The airport is thirty minutes from the hospital, on the south side of the city. After a brief triage, I was admitted to the emergency room to be seen by the doctor on call.

Deepa and Ben were already there. It was so comforting to see them, a blanket for my soul.

I was cold after all this travel and needed an actual blanket as well. These warm blankets are a godsend to patients. They warm your body, heart, and soul. Soon after, David flew in and joined us. David and Ben checked into a Marriott by the hospital, right across the road. Soorya was also on his way to Houston from St. Lucia. He would arrive by midnight after a connection in Atlanta. My white blood cells were proliferating, trying to keep me alive, but so were my people, amassing, gathering around me, a bulwark against bleakness.

After a brief examination, some additional blood work, X-rays, an ECG, and a few other tests, I was transferred to the leukemia floor. It was on the sixteenth floor of a massive, twenty-four-floor inpatient building. There, I was connected to an IV pole so the staff could continue my pain medications and Hydroxyurea. I was subjected to even more tests. My room was rather large, with a sleeper sofa on one side of the room. Like all rooms in the hospital, it had a nice TV, and I had a private phone line. Even the bathroom was bright and spacious.

By early afternoon, Donna had joined us at MD Anderson. She had driven all alone from Baton Rouge. It was a wonderful surprise. Deepa's face opened like the petals of a flower when Donna walked in.

✸

But after that, days and weeks lost meaning and significance, only to be dictated by testing, visits, and hospital admissions. An alternate reality that soon became the norm. The outside world no longer belonged to me. I did a slow dance towards the unknown. My dear wife pushed me through those halls in a wheelchair, as I could not walk. Her strength became mine and saw me through those difficult days. Unable to focus on the terrifying present, my thoughts cast back to my past, images reeled by, startlingly clear.

A Life of Chances

My life has been unpredictable from the start, shot through with as-tonishing beauty and even magic. I was born in a coastal village along the Arabian Sea in the Indian state of Kerala. This southernmost state of India is unique in its geography. It is a narrow stretch of land nestled between majestic mountains and the glimmering turquoise ocean.

Hundreds of small and large rivers crisscross this thin stretch of land from the Western Ghat mountains—which rise up at the very top of the forests—to the Arabian Sea. Large and impressive inland water bodies are spread across the state. These freshwater kayal teem with life and act as water reservoirs, absorbing a protracted monsoon season. Lush coconut plantations to the west and dense tropical forests to the east surround the state in a green embrace. These forests are home to gorgeous flora and fauna. Tigers and elephants roam these mountains and valleys. Hill stations in these mountain ranges are among the most beautiful in the world. The state is home to tea plantations and spice gardens. Called "God's Own Country," Kerala has it all. Year after year, my home region is touted as one of the top destinations worldwide.

People from this region are called Keralites or Malayalees because our language is Malayalam, a close cousin of Tamil, one of the world's oldest languages.

There are two seasons here: the rainy and the non-rainy. The southwest monsoon is the predominant monsoon, which brings torrential rains from the Arabian Sea. This is a perennial gift from the ocean, given over and over since the beginning of time.

Starting every June, massive rain clouds move in from the sea and engulf the land like a dark duvet thrown over a bed. It may rain heavily and nonstop for days with accompanying winds from the ocean.

The first raindrops bring out the sand's distinct aroma, magical and seductive. Many visit Kerala in the first week of June to experience this phenomenon.

This monsoon rain expands to the rest of India, nourishing the land and warming the hearts and spirits of a billion-plus Indians. It is briefly stopped by the Himalayan mountain ranges before it reaches the Tibetan plateau.

The first rainy season extends through September. In these handful of months, the land sleeps. The rain nurtures every living thing. A second rainy season originates in northeast India and the Bay of Bengal. This northeast monsoon begins in late September or October and lasts a month or two. For the remainder of the year, the state is hot and humid, just like the tropics of the Caribbean.

Practically, life stops for days at a time due to the incessant water. Large black umbrellas are synonymous with life in Kerala, and, of course, the sun and the heat when it is not raining.

We lived close to the ocean. Our little seaside village was surrounded by water and had waterways leading to the Arabian Sea. Hence, we grew up listening to the ocean and watching the sun dissolve into its sparklingly blue waters. There was a constant background murmur of waves smashing onto the shore, loudest in the evenings and overnight. These soothing ripples became thunderous during the monsoon season, with huge rollers hitting the shore with tremendous rage. The sound of fishing boat engines was also pervasive, breaking the roar of nature with the occasional mechanical thrum. We often saw sailboats or large ships far out on the horizon.

Our neighborhood is picturesque—romantic and idyllic, a postcard village by the Arabian Sea. The ground is perpetually green, adorned with lush vegetation.

Reigning over all are the coconut trees, planted hundreds of years ago, offering shade from the hot sun. When monsoon lightning strikes these towering trees, they sometimes ignite into fireballs. They were planted in large swaths of land across the entire state by skilled men and women who ensured perfect symmetry, allowing for uniform growth. This creates the illusion of a large, well-planned Mughal garden, but instead of manicured plants, a giant garden filled with tall, graceful trees swaying in the wind, necklaced with round, green coconuts. The effect is an open theatre showcasing a magical dance of tree and sky, choreographed by the never-ending breeze and the rising and setting sun.

A stream passed by our house, quiet and innocent, yet always in motion, its clean water carving ravines that separated houses from the coconut plantations. These ravines were dug up hundreds of years ago for irrigation but added to the landscape's beauty. These fresh waters and their tributaries are home to many kinds of fish. Tall white storks, constantly on the lookout for easy prey, lord over the banks.

The sea breeze rocks the coconut palms eternally. Evenings sparkle like jewels lit by rays of the setting sun, a light murmur of crashing waves in the background. Mornings are heavenly. The sunlight rose-gold, birds chirped and cooing.

The ocean breeze brings a light chill during the winter months, and the days are shorter, but the Arabian Sea is always warm enough to swim without shivering. Migratory seabirds visit like tourists looking for a beach vacation. They stay by the sand and play with the crashing waves on the beach. Pretty but noisy, these yearly visitors sport white coats, which contrast nicely with their red beaks and long, slender legs. Larger than pigeons but smaller than the seagulls I saw in Scotland and London, and much less aggressive. Once, while eating a sandwich by the River Thames in my early days in London, a giant seagull swooped in, snatched my sandwich, and scratched my face on its way out. Since then, I have been careful around them. I am convinced these birds carry the souls of men and women who died angrily and want to punish the rest of us.

The sea birds that visited us in Kerala were harmless and playful and had perfected a dance form while going after the little mollusks burrowed in the sand where the waves broke. With each breaking wave, they would shake their rear ends and run in unison in front of the waves like a charging army, only to turn back and retreat as the waves recede. This dance continued throughout the day, making them hungry. The coconut trees by the shore became convenient and provided sleeping quarters. The migratory birds leave us by mid-March, only to return for the next Christmas season.

Abundant dolphins graced us with their frequent presence. Playful and energetic, they belong to the Indian Ocean humpback dolphin family. Amiable, social creatures, they swim close to the beach without fear. These beautiful creatures were a constant presence on the entire Malabar coast. The fishermen had an age-long understanding and never fished for them. If one was caught in the nets by accident, only then were they sold for meat.

The sea turtles arrived towards the end of the monsoon when the ocean had calmed down. These large leatherbacks reached us yearly and laid hundreds of eggs by the shore, in the sand, away from where the waves broke. Hundreds of baby turtles return to the ocean after they hatch. There were days when people would watch for these turtles to come ashore and steal their eggs, which were then sold in the market as an aphrodisiac. Nature and conservation groups then took over, monitoring the arrival of the turtles. Volunteers took turns babysitting the eggs, waiting for them to hatch. They all turned west to the ocean as if programmed to do so and ran away from the humans. All gone in a matter of minutes.

I have four siblings, including my identical twin brother. We twins are the youngest, with me being born last of everyone. My father, a well-known figure in our community, was the headmaster of my school, akin to that of a school principal in the United States. My mother was also invested in the mission of education as the headmistress and manager of an elementary school owned by the family. We were a middle-class family with a solid foundation built on educating young people.

My mother is possibly the busiest and most hardworking person I have ever known, who nevertheless always found time to help us.

Her father, an educator, died at a young age, leaving behind seven children and a wife, who was also a teacher. As the eldest, my mother had to finish her education earlier than expected to help support the family. Fortunately, her late father had already established a school near their home, and my mother started teaching there at a young age. She retired from the school after serving close to forty years.

Although she only took a one-year primary education course after high school, she could easily handle all of our college coursework. Keeping her finger on the pulse of Indian and world politics, she read newspapers and listened to the radio. She also had the best handwriting one could possibly have!

I never met my paternal grandfather either. He contracted malaria while working on a plantation in Trincomalee, Sri Lanka, and died when my father was seven years old. He was the first person in our family to go abroad. After he left India, my grandmother never saw him again. He was looking for a better job and a better life for his family. At the time, my grandmother was pregnant with her second child. She never remarried, but lived with us and was an important nurturing force while I was growing up. She prayed every morning and evening without fail. During evening prayers, she would read aloud the Hindu scriptures, the Ramayana and the Bhagavad Gita. She also made us children read the scriptures with her.

I grew up acutely aware of the difficulties faced by those around us due to the widespread poverty in our village, which persists to this day. Our family, especially my grandmother, helped many people by giving away books, food, and clothing, as well as by lending money to families in need. We always had servants, many of whom grew up with us. This was a common situation in rural India during the sixties. However, looking back, I believe we could have done better: paid them more and nurtured their dreams.

Our house was two-story, one of the neighborhood's oldest concrete homes. It was a place where people came with their problems and found solutions within our capacity. My eighty-seven-year-old mother still lives there with a nursing aide. Both my mother and the dwelling that nurtured me are still important presences in my life.

I slept upstairs in a corner room shaded by the coconut, mango, and jackfruit trees. I could see and feel the ocean from there. Though we had an air conditioning unit, we never used it because the constant breeze from the sea kept us cool. Watching the monsoons and listening to raindrops on the ceiling was an absolute joy. During the monsoon, this soothing murmur changes to pure rage, which can be quite intimidating for outsiders. The rain lasts for days without a break, and the sun shies away. Ponds and streams would overflow during the monsoon.

My father built our current home as an extension of the old ancestral home with a tiled roof. It stands between a tarred road to the east and a stream that flowed behind the house and into the ocean. To the west of our home, the stream and ocean. We have a well that provides clean drinking water without any salty taste, unlike many nearby houses with non-potable wells.

My grandmother grew vegetables in the large garden near a cowshed. My father occasionally milked in the mornings when the milkmen were away or on holiday. He preferred Jersey cows, an imported breed from the United Kingdom, which produced plenty of milk for our family. My grandmother loved goats and chickens, and they seemed to listen to her and follow her commands.

Of my siblings, I grew up to be the roughest, most careless, and most carefree. I was fearless and unpredictable. I took risks, and trouble often found me. It was in my nature. I occasionally got into fights at school. My twin brother was more measured and more predictable. He had boundaries that he never crossed. That said, he was also an instigator, often urging me to do the things he was afraid to do. He often told on me to our parents.

My twin brother and I routinely climbed the tall coconut trees that grew beside the stream that flowed past our house. Some of these coconut trees slanted toward the water and grew horizontally, spreading outward instead of upward. After climbing these trees, we would jump down into the stream and follow it to the ocean. This was very dangerous. The stream had torrential currents, especially during the summer months when it rained for months at a time, and were difficult to escape. Where the stream met the ocean, the water became even more dangerous with swirling currents and rough waves. Moreover, there were rip currents that could easily pull a person quickly out into the deep ocean. These currents could prove deadly even to the most experienced fishermen, who avoided going into the sea during the peak monsoon months. My brother and I did not fear or care about the potentially deadly consequences. We played in that stream from a young age without our parents consenting, or even noticing.

To the south was an empty coconut plantation and land primarily used for drying coir, the fibrous husks from coconuts. Ravines from the stream crisscrossed this land. There were plenty of fish and the occasional eel.

A tree by the corner of this piece of land bore poisonous fruit. The compound to the east of this plantation belonged to an old lady who lived and died as a mistress of a wealthy local man. She had no children and was hostile to us kids. She kept everyone away except her man, who also had grown old. We feared her, especially as we sneaked in to pick ripe tamarind by a small pond on her property. Famously, local police discovered knives and a machete—murder weapons—in that same pond.

There was a small harbor near our home. My twin and I spent the summer holidays with the local fishermen. Motorized boats were a rarity in those days, and most fishermen had no access to them. Paddling in small wooden rafts all night by the light of a hurricane lamp, these brave men rowed into the depths of the Arabian Sea powered only by their chiseled arms and the prayers of their families for safe return. They cast long nets into the sea, sometimes hundreds of yards deep, for mackerel and sardines, only found in deeper ocean waters.

My twin and I would swim out up to a mile with the fishermen, fighting huge, monstrous monsoon rollers—the fishermen taught us how to break through these ferocious waves and come out on the other side. Out there, the shore looked like a mere speck on the horizon.

I would never venture into such waves now, knowing the danger they pose, juxtaposed with my deep understanding of the fragility of life. But I cheer for my brave, adventurous younger self, who experienced such exhilaration. And who was, it must be said, preternaturally lucky.

Once, a fight between fishermen broke out at sea and made the news—possibly the only time we had made news apart from a cyclone and its attendant large coastal erosion. The fight was between men with motorized boats and locals with their motorless rafts. The two groups attacked each other in the deep ocean waters, and many lost their lives. I was a young teen when I witnessed bodies coming ashore, washed up by the surf, and I avoided that part of the beach for weeks out of fear.

In truth, every monsoon season, the sea claims lives.

The worst storm was in 1977 when I was twelve years old, a remnant of the great cyclone that hit the state of Andhra Pradesh that year and killed approximately fifty thousand people. At the time, there were no warning systems in place, and the tidal waves and cyclonic winds devastated entire towns and villages.

I have very clear memories from this event. The cyclonic winds we experienced shook the coast, and people ran, leaving their houses and possessions behind. It was a truly ferocious sight to behold, and it went on for days. The waves were so violent that even the seasoned, fearless seafarers were frightened. The sea claimed hundreds of meters of land, engulfing homes and properties.

After the wind and monstrous swells had receded, the minister from the state government appeared in person to console the fishermen who lost everything. His white Chevy Impala was the first foreign-made car I ever saw. My father led the reception team and accompanied the minister, showing him the extent of the damage. It made me proud.

Despite all this, the ocean was part of our daily lives, and we spent countless hours swimming in the Arabian Sea. It was my first love, and this little stretch of ocean along the coast of Kerala embraced and caressed me as I grew up.

Clay Pots Covered with Silk

In the fall of 2012, my father died of a sudden stroke. Deepa was with him on that fateful day. I was at my morning clinic in the office when she called in a state of panic. I stepped out to take the call when I knew my father wished to talk to me. During our conversation, my father tried to communicate with me in a faint voice but suddenly had a violent coughing fit and lost consciousness. Deepa screamed, and he was gone within minutes. I took the next available flight to Kerala. By then, his cremation had already taken place. It was performed in our family compound, as is customary in parts of South India.

My father's ceremony was my first experience with the funeral ritual.

The funeral pyre was built with a tree cut down in the compound and chopped into body-sized pieces. People often choose the type of tree for their funerals. My grandmother, for instance, was very clear about the particular mango tree she wanted for her pyre. It stood by the pond in the family compound, just big enough that she could hold her arms around it. It bent horizontally as it grew bigger, with branches dipping into the water as if to drink from the pond. We honored her wish. Her slender body was surrounded by the pieces of the tree she cherished, and together they became ashes on their final journey.

Once the tree is cut and the pyre is prepared, the body is brought to the pyre by the family, who chant prayers for the departed soul. The funeral pyre is then lit by children or close family members while everyone chants prayers. The priest leads the ceremony like an orchestra conductor, with the women of the family standing around the pyre. The fire burns slowly for a day, with the ocean breeze carrying the smoke away.

On the third day after my father's cremation, the male children, us twins and our elder brother, gathered at the funeral pyre to collect the charred remains and ashes, as tradition dictates. We carefully retrieved parts of the skull, vertebrae, and fragments of long bones—the remnants of our father's once-living body. These remains were placed in small clay pots.

With the pots filled, we covered them with a piece of red silk with dark-yellow borders. The cloth bore the eternal Hindu symbol of *Om*, a mark of divinity and supreme consciousness of the soul. The pot carried our father's soul, marking the completion of the circle of life, an acknowledgment of a Universe where we are given life and yearn to return. We wrapped the pot in a small garland made with fresh flowers plucked from our garden. We were careful not to drop the pot or place it on the ground, carrying it overhead until it was time to release the soul into the ocean.

A dark, gloomy sky arched overhead and the sea was especially rough and tumultuous. The ocean appeared dark and clouded with muddy water, the waves' violent motion frothing the surface. Thunderstorms and torrential rains from the northeast monsoon drenched us.

The priest didn't venture into the waves, but my elder brother slowly walked in. My twin and I followed right behind him.

We broke the waves, opened the pots, and sprinkled the ashes and small bones we had collected into the watery depths. After releasing our father's remains, we threw the pots far into the ocean. We repeatedly chanted *Om Namo Narayanaya*, seeking peace and comfort for the departed soul.

My father felt especially deserving of peace. He lost his father at seven. After finishing high school, my father ran away from home in search of work. He found a job as a hotel cleaning boy in a city far from home. He then returned, completed a diploma course, and became a teacher. Soon, he became a well-respected community leader and principal of the school. He was kind, generous, and trusting of people around him, traits that led to trouble toward the end of his life. After retirement, he became the managing director and chairman of a local bank. Unfortunately, trouble soon found its way to the bank. Not his fault, but he couldn't help but feel responsible. This upset him greatly and he started drinking excessively. He soon slipped into rapidly progressing dementia.

The clay pot ritual helped me imagine my father as truly liberated into the Universe through the Arabian Sea, the very medium we had all grown up with. I deeply wish the same for myself when I depart from these shores.

My soul belongs to those waters. The thought is both liberating and exhilarating. This feeling is especially acute now, with the somber reassurance of survivorship so close to me. It crosses my mind many times a day. I can see my dear wife and other family members standing by the water. I can envision Soorya carrying my ashes and walking into the ocean, chanting the same mantra I once did.

Om Namo Narayanaya
Om Namo Narayanaya

Transplantings

Despite my rebellious nature and the interruptions that resulted from dealing with and healing most of the symptoms of Legg-Calve-Perthes disease, I excelled in school. In 1983, soon after I turned eighteen, I embarked on medical school. Even today, an undergraduate degree is not necessary to get into medical school in India. Admissions were purely merit-based, and the competition was fierce. In 1982, when I took the entrance exam, nearly fifty thousand students competed for fewer than six hundred available spots. My twin brother decided to study engineering, and our paths diverged.

My carefree nature followed me into medical school, though I continued to do somewhat well academically. I found a few like-minded friends, and we formed lifelong friendships that remain strong today. My newfound band of brothers and I spent our vacations traveling to different corners of India, trekking through the wilderness.

Once, in the fall of 1988, the police and the military almost sent out a search party to look for me when I was lost in the foothills of the Himalayas for three days. I had gotten separated from my friends on a remote, isolated mountain peak. A native tribal Nepalese family found me wandering in the woods aimless and confused. They escorted me down to their home and fed me, urging me to drink salty homemade tea. I slept for hours out of sheer exhaustion.

When I finally awoke, they took me to the nearest village with a paved road. At the time, guerrilla forces were fighting for independence from India in that region. Many villagers had guns, and they looked at me with suspicion. I was grateful that this family took care of me. Once I reached the village by road, it took me another forty-eight hours to meet up with my friends, who were anxiously waiting.

❀

I practiced rural medicine from 1989 to 1991 before I got married. This is where I got acquainted with death and the countless ways one could die. There are over a billion people in India, and it is equally true that there are over a billion ways to die in India. Living in India will make you realize how imminent and trivial death can be. Death arrives as heart attacks and accidents. In a country with minimal traffic rules, accidents of various forms and shapes rule the day. It is often said that anytime you are on an Indian road, you are taking your life into your own hands. Then there are stabbings, snake bites, and drownings. People get hit by trains or trampled by elephants. Cities with tall buildings become magnets for those who jump. Others are found dead by the roadside, most likely due to alcohol poisoning. Infectious diseases in India are rampant, and the public health system is too bare-bones to effectively tackle epidemics of communicable diseases.

Though suicides seem like isolated events, they too have a "communicable" aspect. They are the all-too-common human tragedy no one talks about. The faces of men, women, and schoolchildren who committed suicide are haunting. Morgues in Kerala are filled with these lost souls. I witnessed many hangings growing up.

Once, I helped bring a body down from a small tree surrounded by darkness in the middle of the night. It was a ghastly experience and was hard to come to terms with. This poor soul was a lady whom I knew from my village. She had at least seven children, all very young. She just gave birth to her last child a few weeks prior. She and her husband argued about her unwillingness to have more children. The children were all sleeping in the hut next to the small tree, oblivious to the loss of their mother.

A knock on the door in the middle of the night mostly meant suicide, snake bite, or difficult labor. One midnight, two men whom I knew came and whispered to me in my ears about the hanging. I soon went with them with my stethoscope. I was supposed to pronounce death, so they came to me. They had flashlights, and I followed them. I was worried about poisonous snakes.

They were scared to bring her body down. It is a crime to do so without the permission of the local police. However, the police never objected to it as they were overwhelmed by the number of suicides. One was her husband, who was in shock.

Her feet almost touched the ground. The light breeze gently rocked her body. It was pitch dark, and even the moonlight hid its devastated face. She wore a creamy white cotton lungi, a garment that women wore from the hip down, and a white blouse with no bra. It looked like she had just breastfed the infant.

On another summer night, while I was in high school, a friend of mine came home and asked for help. He was looking for his mother. She was missing through the night. He lived with his mother; his father was an army officer. They were reasonably well off. He was short in stature, had curly hair, and was very good at mathematics. He also had a small Vespa scooter, a gift from his father. We attended different schools, but we knew each other. We had become friends during special mathematics coaching sessions we attended during the summer holidays. His mother suffered from a form of melancholy. The son told me that she had done these walkouts in the past and had always come home. However, he was more concerned this time as some men had told him she was walking west towards the beach, which was approximately a mile from his house, closer to mine. Hence, he came to me asking for help. He didn't know where to look, didn't want to draw too much attention to the issue, and hoped that she would eventually come home.

There were no streetlights, and it was pouring rain. Most people were asleep. Some fishermen, awake by the beach, were knitting their worn-out nets and smoking beedis. They knew me through my father and told us they had seen a shadow walking into the water. These fishermen often see things no one would believe, ranging from sea elephants to ghosts in the ocean. It was monsoon, which meant the sea was furious and raging with howling winds. I consoled him as much as I could. He went back home all alone in the thick of the night. His mother never returned as he had hoped and prayed for. Her body washed ashore a few miles from our house the next day.

Then there is Sheila, one of our neighbors. Her story is traumatic to revisit, and I had to stop and recompose myself many times. The trauma and sadness are still very real.

Between our house and the stream, there is a house that belonged to my father's uncle, a retired schoolteacher, and his family. Next to their home, the stream flows westward, carrying water and sorrows to the ocean. There were many to be washed off.

Two houses south of our home was Mulangan House, where Sheila lived with her sister and only brother. Some unfortunate things happened there. The brother, who was the oldest, was a type 1 diabetic who struggled with insulin use. He could not stop eating sugar and ended up in hospitals, often in a diabetic coma. In one of those hospital visits, he never made it back. He was in his thirties when he died.

The two sisters were then left to fend for themselves. The most beautiful of the sisters was Sheila, the eldest. A kind soul, she was an excellent tailor and seamstress. By Indian standards, where a light complexion is highly valued, she was considered a true beauty. The local men constantly pursued her, following her on motorbikes and harassing her. As an adult, I'm horrified by this, but it was amusing to me as a kid to see these men trying to get her attention. Somehow, the two sisters managed to make ends meet. My mother helped them financially.

I left the village for my medical studies in 1983 and stayed in medical school till 1990. While working in the Casualty (what Indians and Brits call the ER), I heard a familiar voice. It was Sheila, who had also moved to the city. In addition to her tailoring work, she was a caregiver for an elderly couple. She was with her husband, a construction worker, tall and handsome. I distinctly remember his biceps, those of a bodybuilder. His broad, muscular chest reminded me of movie stars in America. He had a head full of hair, combed in style. He also had a narrow mustache, like a pencil drew it. They told me they were parents to a young child. Both Sheila and her husband's eyes darted around the room, their mouths were tight with tension.

They loved each other, it wasn't that.

Sheila told me that her husband had been bitten by a stray dog, but neither of them had given that much thought at the time. However, recently he began feeling unwell, developed cough spasms, and became irritable and unfocused. He was also unable to sleep and was scared to drink water. That was all I needed to hear. I subtly told Sheila not to touch or hold him close. I asked the nurse to give us a corner room and whispered my concern to the charge nurse. She soon bought me a glass of water. The casualty went quiet, and everyone watched in silence. He panicked at first on seeing the water. Then he tried to take a sip of water on my insistence. He then had a violent cough spasm so uncontrolled that his eyes bulged out. Everyone in the emergency room watched in silence.

I knew I would have to witness the most miserable death, likely to occur within the next few days. It was the worst form of death that could befall someone. I told Sheila I would arrange a taxi, and we would take him to the main campus for further testing and to be reviewed by a senior professor. Soon, we got into a cab and traveled to the main campus. I sat in the front seat next to the driver. I asked Sheila to avoid any physical contact. She sat far away from him in the back seat, wiping her tears with her sari. He seemed to calm down once in the taxi and away from the city limits.

Asking the driver to go slowly. I rolled my window down and watched him from the corner of my eye. He started struggling to breathe immediately and returned to an anxious and agitated state. It was a similar reaction to what he experienced in the casualty. That was the confirmation I needed. The fear and the response to water is called hydrophobia. Just the thought of drinking water or seeing water can elicit violent emotional disturbance and pharyngeal spasms. The reaction to air hitting the face is called aerophobia. Though not as common as hydrophobia, a similar response is highly suggestive of rabies and impending death.

My professor examined him, repeating the test with a glass of water. The nurses brought a fan close to his face. Without a doubt, it was rabies. It was heartbreaking. He sat there emotionless. He knew his days were numbered, and he was not going to see his wife or daughter again. Sheila was devastated.

The charge nurse took over from there. An IV line was started by her and secured with a splint. They changed him into a hospital gown.

Senior nurses at these districts' headquarters hospitals and medical colleges have seen many similar cases and have perfected a drill in caring for adults and children with rabies. Only the most senior nurses were involved in the care. Rabies patients are a significant case in any hospital that treats them. An air of impending doom fell on the hospital and its surroundings. The death is so violent and certain that no one, not even the most advanced hospital in the world, can change the outcome.

Sheila and I walked through a compound behind the casualty. The location was discreet to keep away the spectators. It also ensured that the rooms would have ventilation and that the trees provided shade. The cell had metal bars with no windows; one could see these patients behind the large iron bars. He would soon be confined to a small, dark room, where only the nurse was allowed to visit him. The room, essentially a cell, would remain locked at all times. Nurses were only allowed with attendants, and extreme care was taken when entering the room. Intravenous fluids and sedatives were the only treatments available.

It was heartbreaking to see their separation. Sheila couldn't hug or kiss him. The sadness was beyond words.

I had spoken to the hospital and arranged for her to visit him from a distance. She asked for my presence in those few minutes of seeing her husband. I held her hand and calmed her inconsolable spirit. Fears of contagion were widespread among family members and care staff. Many folk tales about rabies patients flew around in Kerala. One described how these patients would eventually turn into dogs before they died. They would bark, crawl in a confined space, and foam from the mouth.

Sheila visited daily. I waited for her to come and went with her to the visits. She would always hold my hands and cry uncontrollably. Her husband could see her and initially tried to comfort her with words from the cell. They talked about their child, and he wanted to see her. A visit with the daughter could never have happened under these circumstances, in those days. Her visits lasted minutes only, and the staff would lead her out.

The nurses chained his hands and feet to the metal bed by the third day. Copious amounts of foam formed around his mouth in thick quantities. He coughed incessantly, looked at the ceiling, and fought with the shackles.

Sheila would call his name from outside the caged room during the visit. He recognized her voice initially and her visits could calm him momentarily, but towards the end, a violent and continuous cough took over, and he failed to recognize her. His eyes rolled in constant motion. They were fixated on the ceiling as if he were conversing with the roof tiles. It was such human suffering that no one should undergo. The IV drip was placed outside the room and connected to him, so the nurses did not need to enter, and the room was kept dark on purpose. The shade from the trees and the breeze from the courtyard kept the room comfortable.

I waited for Sheila on the fifth day with a heavy heart. He had died the previous night. That was the last time I saw her.

I asked my mom about Sheila and her sister as a part of penning these lines. I feared the answer. My mother sighed. "Sheila moved to Kochi, found work, and had gotten her daughter married off. But I sadly heard that she was doing more than tailoring to care for the daughter," my mom said. I understood what that implied. Sex work. "Sheila hung from the ceiling of the tiny house she had built for herself."

Sheila's sister too, was tall and beautiful, albeit thinner, so she more easily escaped unwanted male attraction. In her late twenties, her abdomen distended and weight fell off her scant frame. I examined her in her home, which was a small two-roomed house with a front veranda. There was no electricity. She had a lamp lit for the night.

I sent her to a surgeon I knew for a biopsy of the lymph nodes, but the result was inconclusive. We feared Tuberculosis, which was widespread, but TB treatment did not help her. She committed suicide a few years afterwards.

Suicide is a universal curse. It is common in America too. Being in the medical profession, I knew too many people who committed suicide in this country. The only difference is how they do it. The method of choice in poor countries like India is cheaper and more cost-effective: eating poisonous fruits, drinking pesticides, jumping off cliffs, or hanging. With its wealth and modernity, America could afford shiny, polished guns, and they did the job in style. Britain, somewhere in between, often turns to booze and Tylenol. The world has no qualms about these souls. They are forgotten and conveniently never mentioned. These kind and beautiful souls deserve a special place in heaven, a place they can call home, where they can be surrounded by others like them. The children can then make friends and play with their kin. A camaraderie of souls. They will be placed on the highest pedestal, above the gods, saints, and royalty, alongside the children killed by violence in the world, especially those slain by guns in America. I fervently hope that the most beautiful of the angels are tending to them in heaven.

Angel of Angels

Deepa. Our lives crossed as if they were destined, our names spelled as if we were meant to be together from birth.

My mom's sister first introduced us in the fall of 1990. The day we met, Deepa had recently awoken and wore no makeup. Her large eyes were bright. Long, silky hair flowed over her shoulders and down her back. She spoke clearly without hesitancy. I thought she was loud, but I felt an immediate spark. I was attracted to her strength and forthrightness.

Deepa was visiting my town from Kannur, six hours away by train. Vasco da Gama visited Kannur in 1488, where he established the first Portuguese settlement in India, thus starting the long foreign occupation of India. The Portuguese built a fort on the cliffs overlooking the Arabian Sea, which still stands. Dutch colonizers followed, and eventually, the British ruled the subcontinent from 1790 until Indian Independence in 1947.

Six hours is far by any standard, and I was busy practicing rural medicine. Even if it had been allowed, I didn't have time for an extended courtship or visits. We grew closer through letters and phone calls.

Deepa hails from a family of doctors. Her grandfather was a doctor in Myanmar, working for the British armed forces. Her father was born in Rangoon, and the family had to escape back to India during the

Japanese invasion of World War II. Both her parents were doctors, her mother and sister both gynecologists. They had built a moderate-sized hospital, primarily for labor and delivery, and practiced in their hometown. Deepa, on the other hand, took a different path. She studied literature and trained to become a teacher.

We were married in May 1991 on a hot Indian summer day. The wedding was held at Deepa's house, as is customary in the Malabar region of Kerala. I was twenty-six years old; Deepa was nearly twenty-four. It was the first Sunday of the month, and the wedding was held outdoors with all the pomp and ceremonies befitting my in-law's status. The groom's party—two busloads of people, as my dad had invited the whole village—had traveled from my place the night before. Many others arrived in cars and trains.

There were over two thousand people in attendance, and it felt never-ending. The sadya, the meal that was served at the wedding, had to match the family's status. My father-in-law had handpicked the best chefs from the state, who cooked the entire night before the marriage. It was a vegetarian meal with over twenty dishes accompanied by fruit and desserts. It was joyous and delicious, but Deepa and I were both exhausted by the end of it. It was dark when we reached my home. We had our first kiss in the back of an ambassador car somewhere on the highway between Kannur and Kozhikode.

But we weren't done yet: the next day was a reception with close to a thousand people in attendance for those who couldn't attend the wedding!

In July 1991, I left Kerala to study internal medicine. The program I entered was a three-year residency, much like the residencies in the United States, at an excellent institution in Mangalore, a coastal southern Indian city known for its cuisine and medical education. My father-in-law had graduated from this institution in the 1950s as part of the inaugural class and had fond memories of his time there.

Mangalore is in the state of Karnataka. It borders Kerala, but Deepa and I were still a three-hour train ride apart. Deepa stayed in Kannur, and I took the train home on the weekends to visit her. This was not an ideal arrangement—Deepa wanted to be with me. We argued over this, but I didn't have the means to find living quarters for us together. I was too proud to ask my parents or in-laws for help. This was a difficult time for both of us. Looking back, I regret the lost time and wish I had found a way for her to live with me in Mangalore.

Two years into my residency, in April of 1993, joy of all joys, Soorya arrived in this world. He had big, bright eyes, a large forehead, and thin, sparse black hair. I was the first one to hold him. He looked directly at me and smiled, and with that touch of magic, we became a family of three.

Deepa and Soorya lived in Kannur for the next year, and I visited as often as possible. In the summer of 1994, I finished my residency and found a job as an assistant physician in Mangalore. I did my hospital rounds, looked after patients in the mornings, and conducted a busy outpatient clinic in the afternoons.

I managed to find accommodation for my family in the heart of the city. It was an upstairs apartment rented out by the family who lived downstairs. It was close to work, and the family downstairs had young children who became Soorya's playmates. For the next year, we lived happily together in Mangalore.

Maiden Voyage

By the summer of 1995, my son, an energetic bundle of joy, was running through the corridors and the rose garden next to our house. I, on the other hand, was restless and wanted to study more. I decided to go to the United Kingdom to further my education. I was hoping to study cardiology. I had no concrete plans for attaining this goal, nor did I do much research into it. This would soon prove to be a disastrous decision.

I decided to take the highly competitive Membership of the Royal College of Physicians (MRCP) exams in the United Kingdom. These exams serve as gatekeepers for specialty training and good training jobs in medicine in the United Kingdom. These exams are historically difficult and challenging, with low pass rates, even for British medical school graduates. Most doctors attempt these exams after a few years of training in the British medical system. And foolish as I was, I had never been to the country, let alone been versed in the training.

The MRCP exams have two parts. The first is a written test of your advanced medical knowledge. Once you pass that, you are allowed to take the second part of the exam, the dreaded clinical exam. In it, you examine up to ten patients in less than thirty minutes and make clinical diagnoses while being observed by two hawkish professors.

Leaving Deepa and Soorya was heartbreaking. We had only been together as a family for one year. But I was determined, and Deepa supported my desire to further my education. In June 1995, we traveled to the British consulate in Chennai, the nearest consulate to Kerala. It was a big deal to secure a visa in those days. A lot depended on luck. There was a large line of applicants looking for a British visa. Deepa stayed outside. The fellow in front of me who was confident about securing the visa got rejected. Then, it was my turn. The visa officer was nice to me and asked various questions about my plan or lack of it. He approved my application and gave me a six-month permit to travel to the United Kingdom.

Soon, I was packing my bags and books to go to London to take the first part of the MRCP exam.

June 18, 1995, was a Sunday. A fateful day in my life. My entry to a new world. The West. With all its history, glory, and shortcomings.

This was my first trip abroad, and I had yet to learn how unprepared I was for it. I had no reservations for a place to stay, nor did anyone wait for me at the airport. I had never dealt with British currency before and carried no credit cards. In those days, there were no cell phones to call someone and ask for help. All I had was a large suitcase packed with books and clothes and enough money in US dollars to last me a month.

In my pocket were a few addresses in a London neighborhood called East Ham. These were families known to sublet to foreign doctors at a subsidized rate where I could find a place to stay. But how to get there?

My flight from India departed Mumbai a few strokes before midnight. I would be traveling back in time.

I traveled aboard a British Airways jumbo jet. In those days, you could smoke on the plane, and my seat was right in the middle of the smoking section. I couldn't sleep on the plane due to the heavy aromas of burning tobacco and bitter alcohol. And, of course, I was nervous about the unknown.

I was tired and hungry when I landed in London. Heathrow Airport, then as now, one of the busiest airports in the world. Once cleared of customs and customary immigration checks, I entered a massive reception area buzzing with the morning crowd. The smell of freshly ground coffee and freshly made bread wreathed the air. There were long lines of people from around the world and little flower shops with beautiful roses as well as flowers new to my eyes. The airport was so well-lit that it appeared like I was in a movie set. It was magical and scary at the same time. Soon after the excitement, an unexpected sadness came over me with the thought that no one was waiting for me at the airport, even though I knew that would be the case.

It was imperative that I reach East Ham in daylight so that I could search for accommodation, never realizing how tired I would be upon landing in London. I had never even heard of jet lag.

I knew about the London Tube, but had no idea how to navigate what looked like a tangle of wires or veins on the station maps. Finally, I figured out that the District line would take me to East Ham, though first I had to board the Piccadilly Line and switch trains.

I grappled with the money exchange and bought a Tube ticket from a vending machine, and watched the crowds as they moved effortlessly through the subway. I finally got onto a train with much relief.

The train was crowded and filled with tourists and daily commuters. After Monument and Whitechapel stations, the train rose to ground level, traversing central London along the Thames, crossing Westminster and many historical landmarks. This was my "Alice in Wonderland" moment—places I'd only read about in books as a kid from a tiny South Indian village became startlingly real.

I can vividly recollect, even today, how I felt as I stepped off the train at East Ham station. A run-down east London township, East Ham is nothing like the London in most movies. Culturally, it is a hemisphere away from Buckingham Palace or the bustling commercial Oxford Street.

Foreign medical graduates from the Commonwealth countries have been coming to England for generations. Most come to London to take the Professional and Linguistic Assessments Board (PLAB) exam, which would allow them to work in British hospitals. They generally stayed in low-income neighborhoods while studying for and taking their exams.

At the time, doctors from South India preferred the neighborhood of East Ham, as it was a predominantly Tamil and Sri Lankan area of East London, and there were many Asian stores. It was, and probably still is to some extent, common for many doctor-students living with their landlord and sharing common spaces, like the kitchen and bathroom—usually only one full bathroom and if we were lucky a water closet (W.C.) with a toilet. I knew of one place with five bedrooms and only one bathroom shared by all the residents!

When I first arrived in East Ham, the subway station was old and dilapidated. I stepped out of the train and took a giant staircase up, which led to a small atrium where one could buy train tickets, which was shabby and miserable. Exiting the station, I got a crash course in London's chilly, rainy weather.

The streets were filthy and poorly kept. Bits of trash littered the ground everywhere. To my surprise, there were very few white people. As I walked down the High Street, I looked around and saw shops with Indian and Sri Lankan names all around me.

I made my way across the road to a grocery shop with a Tamil name. I was not fluent in Tamil by any means, but I could at least hold a conversation and ask for directions. I was looking for an organization called the Madras Medical College (MMC) Library, which is run by South Indian doctors and helps new doctors find cheap accommodations. Though it is called a library, it was actually a run-down house on Gladstone Avenue close to High Street.

The Sri Lankan grocery store owner directed me to the local Hindu temple (the Mahalakshmi Temple) and, on the next block, the MMC Library came into view. In addition to its collection of exam-oriented books, the library had a canteen that served inexpensive meals. I was told the library was owned and operated by a doctor who had never passed the exams and felt the need to help prospective candidates.

The temple also offered free food on the weekends after evening prayers. It was convenient that two temples were offering free meals after worship. The Sri Murugan Temple is a good bit away from High

Street and Gladstone Avenue, and the food was basic, like a bowl of rice, sambhar, and yogurt. Yet, it was as delicious and nourishing as if cooked by devotees in their homes and brought to the temple as an offering—an authentic, home-cooked South Indian meal. As a result, many of us, mostly doctors and new arrivals to the United Kingdom, were all too happy to attend the evening prayers! We knew when the prayers would be over and when the meals would be served, and we timed our lives perfectly to be in attendance.

We also avoided certain streets and carried very little cash with us because we feared being mugged. The cops carried only batons, as is still the case. I had witnessed a home burglary myself and couldn't do much to help the victim.

Once I reached the MMC Library by early afternoon, my next mission was to find a place to stay. I left my heavy suitcase at the library—I was already worn out and jet-lagged. I had a few numbers to call and a few houses to visit. I hoped that at least one would work out. So, I started my search, methodically going by the addresses I had, and knocked on many doors looking for a room to rent. Some of the home-owners, understanding my plight, tried calling their connections on my behalf. A sweet Malayalee lady felt so bad for me and fed me lunch as she made calls, searching for a place for me. All the attempts were fruitless, and I returned to the library almost falling over in my exhaustion.

Back at the library, I ran into an old friend, Dr. Shetty, from Mangalore. Seeing a familiar face and an old acquaintance felt like a true miracle. I had lost touch with him as he had left for London a year before I started planning my trip. He was already living in East Ham and studying for the PLAB exams. He had failed three attempts and was on his last attempt to clear the hurdle. He offered me a place as his roommate, a godsend.

It was a good bit of walking to the other side of town. There was a light drizzle, and despite the summer, it was damp. On the way to his house, Dr Shetty let me use his calling card to contact Deepa. She was relieved that I had reached East Ham and found a friend and a place to stay. Lugging my luggage through the streets of East London, Dr. Shetty joked: "Deepak, what have you packed?"

My one suitcase was mostly stuffed with books to study for the exam.

Finally, we reached Lathom Road. The house he was staying in had a spare bed in a corner room. It faced not only the street, but a junior school with screaming kids. Needless to say, it wasn't quiet. Still, I slept for the next twenty-four hours straight.

The house was owned by a divorced Sri Lankan surgeon with an unfriendly disposition. His two young children came over the weekends. Nearly every time his ex-wife came to pick up their boy and girl, there was an awful argument in the street, full of curse words in Tamil.

He gave us strict orders on how to maintain the place and imposed restrictions on what we could and could not cook. Bacon was prohibited, but chicken was allowed. The beef was expensive, so we never cooked or asked about it.

Luck favored Dr. Shetty in his last attempt to clear the PLAB exam—positive payback from the Universe.

I quickly learned how to live on my own in England. I learned how to cook, clean, and deal with British currency. I learned how to use the public pay phones to talk to Deepa and Soorya. These were prohibitively expensive, so our calls were rare and short. My friend and I shopped in the cheap, no-frills stores and lived off bread and eggs. Once a week, we treated ourselves to homemade chicken curry. We took full advantage of the free meals at the temples. I studied hard and went through all the necessary exam prep.

In July 1995, London was in full bloom. We visited the botanical gardens and the historical sites as often as we could. We picnicked by the Thames and witnessed drugs changing hands at a large underground dance club. By now, I knew how to navigate the streets and the Tube.

People kissed openly on buses and trains, in parks, and anywhere they could, day and night. Women smoked openly. Men kissed men, and women kissed women. WOW, I had never seen that before!

One night, we missed the last train to East Ham and ended up sleeping rough by the entrance to the station on the street, only to be woken by a drunken fellow pouring beer on our heads. It was rightly served chilled.

Days passed, and my new world became dearer.

A month after coming to London, I took the dreaded MRCP exam. The pass rate for part one was only around 25 percent, and after a few days of waiting, I got the disappointing news that I had failed. This was a defining and difficult moment for me. I now faced a decision: I could stay in London and retake the exam or go back home. Unfortunately, I had run out of cash reserves and had a pre-purchased return ticket. My visa could also run out soon.

It was the last week of July. I watched my defeated self boarding the District Line back to West London, switch to the Piccadilly Line, disembarking at Heathrow. Back on a British Airways jumbo jet, which took off for Mumbai. I took a connecting flight to Calicut and landed by nightfall. I shared a taxi with another passenger and came home to Kannur sometime at midnight. I felt defeated as I traveled back to Kerala. Deepa shared my disappointment. Soorya was excited to see me. I had brought him toys and British cookies.

The next few weeks were difficult for us. Deepa had never shown her disappointment, but I could sense it. It was decision time about what to do moving forward. I wasn't ready to give up, though. Being in London had reinforced my desire to pursue British higher education. I wanted to show the world that I could and would continue this journey of studying abroad.

Months passed. I was not working and obviously had no income. My parents and friends advised me against going back to England.

Meanwhile, I was applying to training programs in London and was accepted into one run by Hammersmith Hospital, one of the finest and oldest British hospitals. The diploma course was expensive; I had to pay 13,000 pounds for one year of training, plus living expenses. This was a lot of money at the time. We didn't want to borrow money from our parents, so we sold jewelry and my car. Soon, I was back in the British Embassy in Chennai, looking for a visa to return to London. This time, the embassy staff had grilled me about the course and the finances.

However, my application was approved again. Deepa had mixed feelings but went along with the plan. I promised she could join me when I found a good place to live and settled down somewhat.

I was back in London at the beginning of October of the same year, 1995. This time, finding a place to live was easy. I took the same Tube train back to East Ham and quickly found a place to share with a colleague in West London, close to the hospital. 73 Erconwald Street, next to the East Acton Tube station.

Our room was in a run-down building with a corner shop underneath it. There was just enough space for one cot; however, the owner had managed to squeeze in two single beds, leaving us barely enough space to walk between them. Our rent was one hundred sterling pounds a month, which we split.

The morning I was moving my few belongings and many books into the flat, several members of a construction crew working in the nearby building approached me and warned me about the dangers of staying there. One handed me a knife for protection as I was trying to open the metal door by the street. "Please take it," he insisted. "You will need this."

I politely declined the offer. I was by no means ready for a knife fight in a new country in the middle of the night.

Our first night, people banged on the door, trying to break in. It was scary. Then we got used to it.

We witnessed many fights and alcohol-related shenanigans. The whole area smelled of beer and cigarettes. Prostitution was on full display. Our neighbors were a French couple who screamed at each other in French all night. We had a common kitchen, which we shared with the landlord's wife on the weekends. She often cooked salted fish cakes, making the entire apartment smell of rotten fish.

My roommate was a middle-aged doctor who spent much time crying. He had recently lost his wife in an accident and was grieving. In addition, this was his first trip outside of India. He had no experience with cooking, cleaning, or doing laundry. I soon realized that I needed to be his caretaker.

The winter of 1995 was brutal. It was extremely cold, with freezing winds and snowstorms. The room we shared was exposed to all the elements of nature. The building was so old that it had minimal insulation. The howling wind would sneak in despite all the little tricks we tried. We had a mini heater in the room, which helped somewhat but failed to keep us comfortable.

We were within walking distance of Hammersmith Hospital, where we were training. To get there, we walked along back roads that carried us through the meadows adjoining the notorious British prison, Wormwood Scrubs.

Soorya and Deepa joined me on May 22, 1996. A Wednesday. Soorya had just had his third birthday celebrated at home in Kannur.

I waited for their arrival at Heathrow. The Chennai-London British Airways flight landed on time. I was nervous for Deepa as this was her first overseas trip. I knew that Soorya, being the good kid that he was, wouldn't give her any trouble despite the long flight.

I waited patiently at the receiving hall and saw them coming out. Deepa wore a yellow salwar kameez with pearly beads on it and was pushing a trolley with her luggage. Soorya held onto her dress as he walked just a few inches behind her. She was looking for me. Soon, we found each other, and I could see the relief on her face. Soorya saw me and shied away for a brief moment. I had bought a sandwich for him, and he enjoyed it while we caught up in the reception hall.

Right before their arrival, I found better living accommodations. The new apartment was opposite the hospital on Du Cane Road in West London, 101 King House.

We exited the Tube at Hammersmith station, with its old stone walls and metal facades, its large clock lording over the entrance. Flanking it were flower shops, book stalls, and kiosks selling newspapers and cigarettes. Walkways lined roses and gardenias still in bloom that warm autumn. Deepa found all this magical. Soorya couldn't contain his excitement.

We had a brief ride from the station in the quintessential London black cab to 101 King House on Du Cane Road, the place I'd rented now that my family was joining me. The driver wore a white shirt, black pants, and a black tie. His mustache was unusually plump and black, matching his tie. He wore a gray cap and spoke with a London accent. He was polite and welcoming, a proper British gentleman. The fare was six sterling pounds, including a pound tip.

Behind the apartments was a busy railway track. The Tube's Central line trains rumbled by every five to ten minutes. I had already gotten used to the sound, but Deepa had trouble sleeping through them. Soorya found them exciting and amusing. He spent hours watching the trains go by. He also loved riding the double-decker buses.

Both Deepa and Soorya loved London. They were in a new world they had only imagined or read about. The roads, the cars, the people, the beautiful English meadows, the flowers—they loved it all. Deepa was thrilled to be in London with its history of poetry and literature. She visited Poet's Corner in Westminster Abbey as often as possible. I was excited for them and happy we were reunited as a family.

Soorya quickly started learning English.

Soon, I was looking for paid jobs. Luckily, I didn't have to take the dreaded PLAB exam, thanks to a scheme by the Royal College called the Overseas Doctors Training Program (ODTS), which exempts those who have completed residency training abroad. My professors from Mangalore, who were trained in England, were kind enough to write letters of recommendation for me, and professors from Hammersmith Hospital supported me as well, which secured my exemption from the PLAB.

A trainee doctor in England had a difficult life in those days. Unless we'd scored a year-long or two-year contract with a hospital, one had to look for a new job every six months. As a result, there was a constant move to a new hospital in a new town.

The next six years saw me moving to different cities in Scotland and Wales. My first job was in the west of Scotland in a town called

Ayr. We flew from Stansted in London to an airport near Glasgow called Prestwick. It was a short cab ride to the new hospital, where they offered me free lodging. Ayr was a seaside holiday town. It is a magical little Scottish town with an old, well-decorated high street. These high streets are unique to British towns and cities, where most of the business in the city happens. They are the center of life during weekends and holidays. The famous golf course Royal Troon was close to the hospital.

Soorya began kindergarten, and Deepa made friends. When I began my job in Ayr, I had precisely one hundred pounds left, which I kept as a single hundred-pound bill. Depositing my first paycheck felt like winning the lottery.

When I arrived home from work one day, Deepa was in tears. We looked at each other and said nothing. Soon, I realized that my son had found a small pair of scissors and cut the hundred-pound bill into nearly a hundred pieces. We assembled all those tiny pieces and arranged them on sticky paper like putting a puzzle together. We took it to a nearby bank, wondering whether they would accept it. Thankfully, they understood our predicament and replaced it for the same amount.

I worked in a small town near Edinburgh for the next six months before moving our family to Wales, where I worked for the following five years. The main hospital was in an ancient Welsh town called Abergavenny, one of the most beautiful places on earth, and I also saw patients in the nearby town of Newport and the capital city, Cardiff. The town of Abergavenny is landlocked among three mountains--the Skirrid, the Blorenge, and the mighty Sugar Loaf—surrounded by sprawling, never-ending meadows that slope down from the peak. Wild horses roamed these slopes, wandering aimlessly in herds, drinking from small, pristine mountain lakes. Spending an evening on these mountaintops, watching these beautiful animals and how they created living, breathing art through their simple existence, feels magical.

The gentle Usk River flowed through the town without any fanfare. It meandered gracefully, crisscrossing the city and its scenery, with numerous small stone bridges showcasing ancient building techniques.

I fished for bass in the river and taught Soorya how to do the same. A traditional Welsh inn graced the northern shore, featuring a wooden deck and patio that overlooked the lush meadow. It was here that I spent many evenings watching the river pass by. We explored many castles and abbeys all around this magical town, which also attracted many German and Scandinavian visitors in the summer.

Eventually, I completed the dreaded MRCP exams and specialized in cardiology. Soorya started his primary school education in Wales. During our holidays, we traveled throughout Europe with ease. A few hours' drive in the morning took us to Folkestone in Kent, where we boarded the Eurostar train, which transported us and our car to Calais in France via the Channel Tunnel, a remarkable achievement. After exiting the tunnel, we drove straight into a French highway, which was initially nerve-wracking as we adjusted to driving on the opposite side of the road.

We made many lifelong friends. Yet, something was missing. My professional life had hit a brick wall. While I was able to specialize in cardiology, my chances of becoming an attending cardiologist were remote. I did very similar work as an attending cardiologist but was paid much less. The renowned National Health Service (NHS), despite its merits, relies heavily on foreign medical graduates yet is unwilling to offer them decent wages. These low-wage positions were almost exclusively reserved for foreign graduates as a cost-cutting measure, with minimal benefits and no prospects for career advancement, leaving many in dead-end roles. As the years passed, I became increasingly unhappy with my lack of professional mobility in the United Kingdom.

I longed to return to Kerala. The bond was very much alive despite the distance, growing stronger as the years not living there accumulated. We visited often, sometimes more than once a year. Deepa missed her family and friends dearly.

The Americas

As the millennium came and went, I grew even more professionally restless. Our options were to return to Kerala and join my in-laws at the hospital they had built or to go elsewhere.

In the spring of 2001, I went to Florida for a cardiology conference. This was my first-ever trip to the United States. I was blissfully unaware of this country's might, breadth, and heart till then. I stayed at a hotel on International Drive in Orlando. Being naïve and foolish, I rented a car on arrival. Unsurprisingly, I struggled driving and nearly caused a wreck on the first day. The roads were vast, and cars were big, bold, and fast. The traffic signals looked different. I somehow managed to reach the hotel without causing a major catastrophe.

At the conference, I met with a few friends who had already left the United Kingdom for the United States. What I saw happening in cardiology in the United States inspired me. Their recommendation and my desire for change led me to take the US licensing exams that year.

This was another risky move. I would have to start my training all over again in the United States. I was already thirty-five years old. There was no guarantee that I would get into a good academic training program. There was even less of a guarantee that I would get into a cardiology program, as they were always highly sought after. Getting the proper family visa was also a challenge in those days. Then, there was the issue of relocating my family. We had already made many good friends in the United Kingdom. I was two years away from becoming a British citizen. The United States was even farther away from our parents and families in India than the United Kingdom. Many of my friends and family advised against the move.

Despite the risks, in October 2001, I went to New York for interviews. I stayed with one of my best friends, Radha (Dr. Satheesan), on Long Island, who was a surgical resident at Maimonides Medical Center in Brooklyn. He had been my partner-in-crime in medical school in India and was part of my band of brothers. The last time I saw him was in 1991. His wife was also training as a surgeon in the Bronx. It was wonderful to catch up while staying with him and his family.

I visited the 9/11 site and paid my homage. The catastrophe was all too recent, and there was still dust everywhere in downtown Manhattan. Fumes were still billowing out of the ashes at the World Trade Center. The city was covered in torn pieces of paper, which stretched into Brooklyn, across the river from Manhattan. The wind tunnels created by the high rises of Wall Street carried torn pieces of paper along with the fallen maple leaves. The charred dreams of many New Yorkers were among them. The Trinity Church of Wall Street, which stood across from the World Trade Center, was covered with heartfelt pleas from those looking for loved ones. Every inch of the chapel was covered in these hastily written pleas with photographs of the missing. The chapel stood as a solace in an ashen land, a tomb of divinity, where lost souls could congregate in their desperate searches for the hoped-for, but there were few answers back. Silence echoed loudly.

I had many interviews and discovered doors opened to me due to my prior experience in the United Kingdom. American program directors loved that I had passed the MRCP exams, which they knew were more challenging than American board exams. Despite the long gap between my college graduation and taking exams, I performed very well on the American licensing exams. I received personal invitations from program directors and chairmen of places like the Mayo Clinic and Yale University. My friend took time off and drove me to nearby hospitals in

Connecticut for interviews. Ultimately, I chose the same training program my friend was in. It was fitting for a friendship that by now had spanned close to twenty years.

I wanted to be in New York, and the program offered the right family visa I was looking for. The program offered me a position outside the traditional Match process in the United States, which would have meant waiting until March of the following year to learn about my employment and visa status if I had a job offer. This process is generally very anxiety-inducing, and given my circumstances, I wanted to avoid the stress. I accepted this pre-match offer from the Chairman of Medicine at one of the busiest training programs in the United States.

The hospital, Maimonides Medical Center, is named after one of the most famous and revered Jewish philosophers and physicians of the Middle Ages, Moses Maimonides, and in fact, the neighborhood ringing the hospital housed the largest population of Hasidic Jews outside of Israel. The hospital and its patients reflected the diversity of Brooklyn, serving local Russian, Hispanic, Arabic, and Chinese New Yorkers. At any given moment, multiple languages echoed through the halls, with more than half of the patients not speaking English. We were continually in search of translators.

In June 2002, I said goodbye to all my British friends and hospital staff. The night before I left for New York, the doctors and nurses threw me a large send-off party—they were sad to see me go. I too felt apprehensive about leaving this great country for the unknown, as did Deepa and Soorya.

The United Kingdom had taught me advanced Western medicine and allowed me to practice with joy. Here, I became a cardiologist, practicing in modern Cath labs and learning to implant pacemakers. Trained by some of the best cardiologists, including European and global leaders in cardiology and echocardiography, my friends and colleagues were a joy to work with. The friendships we formed here have lasted, with many friends visiting us in the States on many occasions. The United States, by contrast, provided more opportunities for professional development, which is understandable, considering the vast difference in size and population between the two countries.

I arrived in mid-June that year to arrange lodging and prepare for our stay. I had to attend an orientation course before the official start date of the program. Soorya and Deepa soon followed me and arrived at JFK Airport on the 26th. Another fateful Wednesday in their lives. Their entry to yet another new world.

The United States of America. With all its history, glory, and shortcomings. They had never been to the United States before. The Virgin Atlantic flight landed late into the evening. I waited anxiously for them. It felt exactly like waiting for them at Heathrow in May of 1996. This time, we took a yellow cab with a Bangladeshi driver.

We didn't speak much on the ride back to the apartment. Of course, they were happy to see me, but there was also an air of anxiety on their faces. Both were tired from the long journey from Wales. The mother and son were once again thrust into the unknown, beginning a new chapter in a new country. It is a difficult task—possibly the hardest thing a family can endure—and my family has had to face it over and over again.

By then, I had arranged basic amenities. The hospital subsidized the two-bedroom apartment. It was a corner apartment with a clear view of the Atlantic Ocean, the harbor, and the tall ships that passed under the Verrazano Bridge. We could also see downtown Manhattan. On clear days, we could glimpse the Empire State Building from our front window.

New York was in the midst of a long recovery, slowly healing from the aftermath of 9/11. Many of the hospital's employees had lost loved ones in those attacks. Maimonides Medical Center in Borough Park, the largest in Brooklyn, had prepared for a mass casualty event. Though that hadn't arrived, the hospital soon faced the reality of many employees losing spouses, partners, and other family members. Most were police, firefighters, and EMT responders who had rushed across the bridge to help.

The sudden transition from the subtlety and naïveté of the Welsh countryside to the harsh, loud, and raw environment of inner-city

Brooklyn was jarring. Brooklyn's intensity and brashness were unlike anything we had ever experienced before. There was constant honking, yelling, screaming, and varying grades of profanity shouted in different languages from all corners of the world at any time of day or night. This was not the America we knew or even imagined. It was truly a shock.

I began my internship in the Internal Medicine Residency Program in July 2002. At work, I found myself at the bottom of the ladder again, taking orders from much younger residents fresh out of medical school. I had worked as a consultant in the United Kingdom, giving orders to house staff. This felt like a fall from grace and was difficult to cope with. Instead of performing catheterizations and implanting pacemakers, my days were now spent drawing labs and conducting digital rectal examinations. Interns in America are at the lowest rung of the hierarchy, often receiving little respect, and subject to the demands of everyone above them. I coped by using humor to downplay my feelings: "From heart catheters to Foley catheters." It did not help at all.

Deepa had difficulty adjusting to apartment life as we lived on the ninth floor of the Brooklyn building. There were constant howling winds from the ocean, which initially terrified her. She missed her friends. She had to rebuild a life here for us from scratch. Soorya had to adjust to a new school and way of learning. The summer of 2002 was hot in New York. We were not sure that we would last in Brooklyn. Deepa didn't unpack for six months. She prayed that I would change my mind about this course of action and decide to return to the United Kingdom.

After our initial months of culture shock, we slowly adapted to life in Brooklyn and began to love the city. At work, I was soon appreciated by my superiors. The late Dr. Edgar Lichstein, a towering figure and a true New Yorker, was my chairman. He took me under his wing and shortened my residency to two years. The program director was the late Dr. Malcolm Rose, a United States Air Force veteran and New York City–trained cardiologist who had himself been born at Maimonides Medical Center. A true humanist and gifted teacher, he became a personal friend. I was then offered the chief residency. However, before

I began this responsibility, Dr. Jacob Shani, the chairman of cardiology, welcomed me to his division as a fellow. My worries about obtaining a cardiology position ended with a brief visit to him in the Cath Lab on a Monday morning in June 2004. Soon, I would be a chief fellow in cardiology, and in 2008, I would complete my training with an additional fellowship in interventional cardiology.

❀

Soorya grew up to be a gentle and kind young man. We forged lifelong friendships in Brooklyn. Ultimately, our time in Brooklyn proved to be a pleasant surprise after an unsure beginning.

When it came to job hunting, I initially wanted to stay in the tri-state area. I visited a few practices in New Jersey and Connecticut. My own program offered me a job. But then, I received an offer to visit a practice in a small town outside Lafayette, Louisiana. The offer came through an old friend who was already practicing in Louisiana. He worked under the umbrella of a nationally known cardiology program based in the area. He was happy with his job and the opportunities he had.

My only knowledge of Louisiana came from visiting New Orleans in 2004, about a year before Hurricane Katrina hit. I had just heard of Lafayette, Louisiana, then. I decided to visit the place and evaluate the practice firsthand. Deepa and Soorya accompanied me on this trip to yet another different world.

The small-town warmth was palpable from the moment we got off the plane. The staff of the practice and hospital welcomed us with open arms. It all felt so different from Brooklyn. We visited the practice and had dinner with the cardiologists and staff. We also met up with our friend from New York.

After two days in Louisiana, we returned to New York. We discussed the place and the position along the way. Deepa was unsure about relocating, as she now loved the city very much—New York does that to you. She had made friends in the schools where she taught. Soorya also wanted to stay in New York. He was greatly surprised by the lack of diversity in the schools he had visited in Louisiana.

Soorya decided to stay in New York to finish his last two years of high school. Deepa would stay in Brooklyn with him until he started college. Then, she would join me.

To make my decision, I tried to calibrate the unhappiness of being far from my family for two long years with pragmatic professional development. I wanted to continue to expand my skill set and learn new procedures and techniques, especially working in other areas of the body outside the heart, which was highly likely in this job. In those days, when you came out of the cities to practice in suburban or rural settings, opportunities for learning and growth were plentiful. New York and the Northeast jobs would most likely offer little personal or professional development. There are already so many doctors of all stripes in this region. Financially, it also made good sense. I was neck-deep in debt, and this job offered me a significant sign-on bonus and substantially higher compensation than what I could get if I stayed in the Northeast.

It was a difficult decision. Still, for me, there was a certain human appeal to what I saw and experienced there. It reminded me of the village where I grew up.

On my second visit, we were looking for an apartment in Louisiana. Soon after, on July 8, 2008, I started working in that small-town district hospital twenty miles north of Lafayette.

I was in the heart of Cajun country. The town and people charmed me. The food, music, and way of life were all new to me. The French-speaking Cajun people migrated from eastern Canada as refugees in the eighteenth century. They set up houses and farms along the Mississippi River and the bayous around it. They brought with them a unique culture. Life was celebrated with ample food, music, dancing, and cold beer. There were frequent communal cookouts. The food was mostly French or Creole, a blend of French, Caribbean, and African influences. There was happiness in the air. Many of my older patients spoke only French.

I commuted from Lafayette to New York on alternate weekends.

Some days, I would leave New York in the morning and be seeing patients in the clinic by noon. Every other Friday saw me leaving the office around one o'clock and catching a 5:30 flight from New Orleans to New York. It was a hectic time.

Soorya finished high school in 2010, and Deepa joined me that summer. By then, I had moved from Lafayette to Baton Rouge. I had been given the opportunity to lead a new cardiology program right outside the city in the town of Zachary. It was close enough that I could live in Baton Rouge. One of the most dramatic and special places I've called home because of what happened to me there.

Days Without End:
The Valley of the
Shadow of Death

Soon after I arrived at MD Anderson, I was transferred to the sixteenth floor of the inpatient building. It was one of two floors dedicated to leukemia. I was on the northeastern side of the floor. This was a large floor with an atrium, elevators in the middle, and wings on either side. The rooms themselves were large and spacious. Everything here was focused on leukemia care and treatment, and the nurses and staff were experts in caring for patients like me.

Apart from the ER physician who screened me when I arrived, I saw no other specialists that first day. I will meet with the leukemia physician the next day. The day went by fast. David and Ben searched for places for Deepa to stay. They looked at a multitude of places around the hospital and finally agreed on the Rotary House hotel. That decision turned out to be a blessing for Deepa. Donna spent the evening with us before checking into her room at the Rotary House. She offered to pick up Soorya from Houston International when he arrived. He finally landed at midnight, and Donna was there to greet him at the airport. Deepa was relieved to see him, and so was I. He hugged us both. He brought us hope and strength when we needed it. I stayed connected to my medicines and IV fluids.

As promised, the leukemia doctor came by the following day with his entourage during the morning rounds. At MD Anderson, morning rounds usually involve a leukemia or transplantation doctor as a team leader. The team also includes a nurse practitioner or physician assistant who works directly under the specialist. A highly trained pharmacist who is well-versed in chemotherapy and managing sick patients is also part of the team. These pharmacists play a vital role in cancer treatment, as chemotherapeutic medicines are individually tailored to the patient and can have a vast number of side effects and interactions. They need to be prepared and stored differently from other medications. They are also infused individually at different rates. Leukemia patients receive multiple chemotherapeutic agents simultaneously, making the process even more complicated. Only a highly specialized team can manage these challenges. Other members of a patient's cancer treatment team are a physiotherapist, an occupational therapist, a social worker, and a registered nurse. On occasion, a clergy member is also involved.

Before meeting with my team, I met with my social worker to ensure I had all the proper insurance approvals.

Deepa and Soorya were with me for the morning visit with the MD, as were David and Ben. Donna waited downstairs in the lobby.

The specialist who saw me was originally from South America and was very pleasant at that first meeting. He recommended further testing, including repeated bone marrow testing. He then discussed chemotherapy and its possible side effects. He answered all our questions, but since this was our first consultation, we didn't get into the nitty-gritty of treatment.

The specialist seemed overwhelmed by the number of people in the room and the barrage of questions from my concerned, medically trained friends.

Soon, though, the crowd dispersed, leaving the three of us alone. I was still nearly silent. That is my way of doing things: letting the system take care of the details. I also knew my limitations, as my knowledge in the field of leukemia was limited and outdated. Deepa was also silent. She looked scared. Soorya sat next to her and held her hand.

The only question I asked the specialist was whether I could complete my initial treatment at MD Anderson and continue my treatment in Baton Rouge. He said that it all depended on how I responded to the treatment. That was when he mentioned that I might need a stem cell transplant, which would prolong my stay at MD Anderson. The refrain "a clearer picture after further testing" was a song that offered rote hope. This is no one's fault; it's the way medicine does the best it can without false promises.

Looking back, I realized I had little idea what I was getting into. I assumed that my time at MD Anderson would be relatively brief and straightforward and that I would soon be able to return home and complete my treatment there. However, I learned that treating leukemia is a long, drawn-out process. It can last from months to years—presuming you live that long and do not succumb to the disease or the complications of its treatment.

The goals of treatment vary with the type of leukemia. Many variables are involved in successful treatment. Without treatment, death is a certainty. With modern chemotherapy and stem cell transplantation, a cure is possible. But even with the most advanced modern medicine, there is still a substantial risk of death.

First, the patient must undergo a very intensive regimen of chemotherapy, which is called Induction of Remission. At this stage of treatment, various combinations of highly toxic chemotherapeutic medicines are given intravenously for a week to ten days. This will likely kill all leukemic cells in the blood and bone marrow. There are various chemotherapy regimens, which are chosen and tailor-made depending on the type of leukemia being treated. In selecting a course of chemotherapy, doctors must take into consideration the patient's age and ability to withstand such intensive and toxic regimens. Doctors will also perform a chromosome analysis of the bone marrow to check for any abnormal genetic mutations before chemotherapy begins. This can help determine the precise nature of the chemotherapy needed. To a certain degree, it can even predict the outcome of treatment. These mutations, which are identified through genetic testing, can also predict one's chances of having the disease return, the dreaded "relapse."

This initial round of chemotherapy should kill all leukemia cells and their precursors in the bone marrow. However, this also means that regular cell production is halted for a time. A person's white blood cell count could fall to zero or close to zero, putting them at risk of serious, life-threatening infections. Blood transfusions are essential during this period, as one's bone marrow is not capable of producing new blood cells. The patient will lose their hair and appetite and also experience significant nausea while undergoing chemotherapy. Fever is also common.

Due to the risk of infection, patients undergoing intensive chemotherapy are under strict isolation protocols. These protocols vary from institution to institution and can last between four and six weeks, depending on the bone marrow's speed of recovery.

The next few days were spent on various tests. I essentially walked the halls as I was told to do. Deepa and Donna sat in the room or atrium. Soorya tried to study in between chores as asked by his mother.

On March 3rd, a few days after I arrived at MD Anderson, I underwent a second bone marrow biopsy. My white blood cell count had normalized by this point, so the Hydroxyurea was discontinued. There was also a significant improvement in my pain levels, and I was able to wean myself off opiates and other pain medications. With my pain decreasing, I was able to get up and walk around the halls more frequently. Intravenous fluids continued, though, so I had to wheel my IV pole along with me. These IV poles are a companion to those of us who receive chemotherapy. They become an extension of your body, and you soon learn to live with them. They are the poles of healing and recovery. The more medicines you have hanging on your pole, the sicker you are or the more intense your chemotherapy is. One must learn to maneuver these heavy poles through the corridors of the cancer wards, trying not to entangle the IV tubing and not bump into other poles and nurses. Soon, I will master this fine art form—the pole dance on the cancer floors!

My second bone marrow biopsy results also revealed a considerable number of blast cells in my marrow. A normal marrow will have as many as 5 percent blast cells. My marrow had 63 percent blast cells, indicating that it is now producing mostly cancer cells. The molecular and chromosome analysis results also came back around this time. They put my leukemia in the "moderate risk" category. Somewhat aggressive, but not aggressive enough to be called high risk. A low-risk category would have been ideal and what I was hoping for.

My care team now had all the information they needed. It was time to start my treatment in earnest.

On March 6th, I started a chemotherapy regimen that would wipe out my leukemia. My specific chemotherapy regimen included a combination of highly toxic medicines—Cladribine, Idarubicin, and high-dose ara-C—that would soon wipe clean my bone marrow. Soon, it would wipe out not just the bone marrow but nearly my entire living self.

I was still attached to an IV pole that fed me a continuous infusion of fluids and chemotherapy medicines. I would receive these chemo medicines for five days, and my bone marrow would be suppressed within a week. After that, I would be transferred to an isolation floor. Until then, I was allowed to walk around the premises and go to the observation deck on the hospital's twenty-fourth floor.

I enjoyed going up to the observation deck, which has a splendid view of South Houston and the world-famous Texas Medical Complex. One can see a multitude of roadways and highways winding through the city, as well as Herman Park and the canal that runs through the park. It is a beautiful sight. On the other hand, watching life go on outside the walls of the cancer hospital often brought on a feeling of sadness. It was a reminder that, somehow, my life had become different from those outside these walls. It was hard to comprehend. While others were driving to work or spending time with their families, I was fighting to survive and keep my family intact.

Cancer became my constant companion, teaching me to learn to live with it as one of the many hundreds languishing in the halls and verandahs of the hospital. Many families often gathered on the observation deck. The deck had a piano, and seeing and hearing people sit and play it was common. There was also a coffee station and snack bar, adding to the ambiance. Despite these attempts to foster a cheerful environment, there were plenty of tears, soft cries, and visible anxiety on faces. No one spoke much; they just waved at each other with an expression of kindness.

Curiously, I found that being surrounded by so many people struggling with the same disease brought a certain level of comfort. I had become a member of a tribe, a fraternity. It was a connection defined by a common purpose and singular aim: to stay alive, to not give in to the ever-present threat of death that followed us all like a shadow.

I spent a lot of time on the observation deck while I still could. I knew that, soon, I would not be allowed outside anymore.

One day, while standing on the deck, watching life move past me, I started writing my final plans. I was alone up there, as I needed to be for such things. As I listened to someone playing the piano behind me, I pulled out my phone and typed up my final wishes. It was surreal. I would cry, write a few words, and then stop writing when I couldn't see through my tears anymore. I would recompose myself and write a little more, only to choke up again. Slowly but surely, I composed a few paragraphs, all while watching life go on around me as usual.

I wanted to be cremated in Zachary, Louisiana, my new home. I didn't want any heroic measures to keep me alive. I wanted a decent and normal death, in peace, at home, surrounded by my wife and son. I wish to hold their hands as I transition. The windows will be open for my soul to leave the body and pass my energy into the Universe. Ancient Shiv mantras will be played in the background.

My ashes would then be carried back to my village by my wife and son. It would then be sprinkled in the Arabian Sea with my family and friends in attendance. It would be a sweet reunion and final homecoming for me, granting my soul eternal peace. I wished that Soorya would carry my ashes to the ocean in a clay pot covered in silk, just as I did for my dad. This pot would then be decorated with fresh wildflowers from our family compound. I hoped that he would be led to the sea by my twin and our older brother. I wished for him to chant *Om Namo Narayanaya* as he sprinkled the ashes into the crashing waves. It would be so comforting to lie in the sea's arms again.

When I was done, I sent these final wishes to a close friend. In the coming days and weeks, I would write more after-life plans for my wife and son. I was still deciding whether to discuss these plans with Deepa or Soorya.

Soon after starting chemotherapy, I started experiencing nausea and lost my appetite. Storm clouds were moving in just as monsoon rains in the summer. I could see that from a distance. My life wouldn't be the same again.

On March 8th, two days after starting chemo, my white blood cell count hit rock bottom. From that point on, I was strictly confined to my room to prevent infection. The next day, my care team decided to transfer me to the isolation floor, called a "protected environment" (PE). The ensuing days and weeks would scar my soul.

Life on the Isolation Floor: A Caged Soul

Deepa packed her belongings. Soorya had already left for the Caribbean, and Donna returned to Zachary. It was just us two now.

She held my hand as the trolley took the elevator down to my new place.

I was not looking forward to this transfer. We had already toured this floor while I was on the leukemia floor. A senior nurse took us down to explain the isolation protocols there, and we were allowed to enter a room and inspect it briefly. I dreaded these small rooms, which seemed more like cubicles than proper rooms. I would be allowed no contact with Deepa or Soorya other than phone calls, even though this is when I would need them the most. I wished they could be around me and hold my hand as I went through the most difficult and challenging time in my life. Instead, I found myself alone in an isolation room. It was just me, a few of my belongings, phone, iPad, and books. All my belongings needed to be sanitized before they were brought into the room.

Deepa watched me through the glass doors that separated us. She seemed so far away. She cried like a child as I was led into my cubicle.

I knew the days and nights ahead would be difficult and long for us. My care team expected me to be in isolation for about a month. There was a significant risk that I would die alone in isolation from the complications of my treatment.

The rooms on the isolation floor of MD Anderson were tiny and cramped, and there were no bathrooms. Instead, I was given a commode. Baths were not allowed. I was given sterile wipes with which to wipe and clean my body. Shaving was not allowed; brushing my teeth with a soft-bristled toothbrush was. Families and visitors were not allowed in my room at all. Instead, right outside my room was a small alcove with a glass window looking in. Deepa stayed there throughout the day; we spoke over the phone. She was not allowed to stay there overnight, so she returned to the Rotary House Hotel to sleep. She was always back in her spot by the window first thing in the morning.

Watching my dear family, friends, colleagues, and staff come and go outside that window, I felt like a caged animal in a zoo, especially when visitors stood outside the room and peered in through the glass. It was a strange feeling, and I wondered about patients with rabies-like Sheila's husband, locked down with no outside contact in a cage-like room. How horrible it must have been—to die alone, locked in a cage.

Soon, the true drama of intensive chemotherapy began to play out. Alone in a dark room, hooked up to IV poles, with catheters poking into my body, and fighting for my life with no privacy, I saw the cruelty of cancer. It was both mental and physical. I realized then that cancer would strip me of my dignity. In isolation, I lost all sense of self-worth. Any pride I had was washed away. I would not emerge unscathed.

I often thought that it would be a true rebirth if I made it through this.

Thankfully, hair loss was not a problem for me: I have been bald since my early thirties and am used to shaving my head. For many, hair loss is devastating and a constant reminder of cancer. It is the ultimate symbol of a patient's lost pride and dignity, often leading to severe emotional turmoil, anxiety, and fear of the unknown.

While I was in isolation, my platelet count dropped dangerously low, putting me at serious risk of internal bleeding—including brain bleeds, which could be fatal. The normal platelet count is between 150,000 and 450,000. Mine dropped to a mere 10,000. Due to my low platelet count, I developed multiple blood spots, called purpura, on my torso. These look like purplish-red rashes caused by blood leaking from the capillaries. I needed multiple blood transfusions and various courses of antibiotics.

By March 15th, I had developed a fever with chills. This fever continued for weeks. I had significant neutropenia—a severe lack of certain types of white blood cells that fight infections caused by bacteria—and bacteria began to grow in my blood. My PICC line—a large catheter inserted in my arm that gives doctors direct access to the veins leading to the heart—became infected and had to be removed. I developed a blood clot in the veins in my neck. With the guidance of infectious disease doctors, I then started with a course of the most potent antibiotics.

Despite these medications, I was also diagnosed with E. coli septicemia the next day. My temperature spiked to 103 degrees Fahrenheit, and my blood pressure dropped suddenly. My heart rate spiked. I had taken a turn for the worse and was in a state known as septic shock. I had severe and continuous rigors and had to be resuscitated at one point. Luckily, this happened during the morning rounds, and my care team was nearby, so they were able to come to my room immediately. The leukemia chief happened to be present, and he held my hand.

He gave orders for intravenous steroids and IV fluids to be pumped into me, and he changed my course of antibiotics. He promised me that I would be fine soon.

Even with all this activity around me, I felt peaceful. My pain decreased. The nurses covered me in blankets as I drifted away, and I felt like I was wrapped in a cloud of delicious calm.

On March 17th, I started having severe rectal pains due to the formation of an internal abscess on my rectum. The doctors assumed this was the source of the E. coli bacteria in my blood culture. This abscess caused me to have constant fevers for days at a time. I developed shingles on my back despite being on antivirals. It was extremely painful, especially since I had to lie on my back in the hospital bed.

Throughout, my nights were long and sleepless. I had severe headaches, which were relentless. Nausea was also a constant companion despite the medications used to thwart it. Sometimes, it felt as though

I was living in a body entirely different from the one I had known my whole life. I was losing weight at a rapid pace. I had stopped eating. My complexion has changed as my body hair fell out.

On March 20th, my care team decided to give me a white blood cell transfusion. These white cell transfusions are rarely used and only in extreme circumstances for patients with severe sepsis who are not responding to aggressive antibiotics. Deepa and I have the same blood type, so she was able to donate her white cells to me. Ben and several of my staff and managers came by and donated. By the last week of March, I had already had two white blood cell transfusions and needed a third.

To donate white blood cells, the donor is first given a medication called Neupogen, which activates the bone marrow and stimulates it to produce white blood cells. The next day, their blood is collected in a blood bank, and the white cells are separated. These white cells appear yellow and frothy, have a short half-life, and must be transfused within a few hours. Like my donors, I also received injections of Neupogen to stimulate white blood cell production.

These white blood cell transfusions almost always elicit significant allergic reactions and fevers in the recipient, and I was no different. I vividly recall one particularly severe allergic reaction after midnight on March 29th. Immediately after I received the transfusion, I started having violent chills and rigor. My temperature soared to over 103. My nurse, a middle-aged Filipino woman, struggled to control my fever. She ended up placing bags of ice all around me. I spent the night soaking wet, packed in bags of ice, wide awake, and in pain and distress.

The headaches that followed were splitting and lasted an entire day.

I spent my waking hours listening to audiobooks. This way, I learned much about world history, especially American history. I learned about the Lewis and Clark Expedition and their journey west to the mouth of the Columbia River. I could almost feel their excitement upon reaching the Pacific Ocean. I learned about the Native Americans and the tragedy they experienced with the arrival of Europeans. I learned about the Civil War and the Revolutionary War.

My friends FaceTimed me from remote lands. Through them, I saw the Great Wall of China and Machu Picchu. I saw Mount Fuji from my bed. I traveled on a bullet train in China with David and watched the rural countryside pass by. I visited the Museum of the Terracotta Army in Shaanxi, China, as Craig Walker, my senior colleague, Face-Timed me.

Fearing the worst, I continued to write after-life plans for Soorya, offering him advice on how to move forward without me. I asked him to take care of his mom and for them to look out for each other. I also continued to write notes for my dear wife on moving forward with her life. She would be financially okay as her parents had already left a significant inheritance to her, including the hospital. Our apartment in Brooklyn is completely paid off. I had life insurance policies amounting to millions of dollars, which I had purchased while in residency, and there were other investments, too. This gave me comfort that she wouldn't have to struggle. All I asked was for her to move forward fearlessly and independently. I asked that she continue my charitable work and the foundation I started in India. I offered short statements and pointers on life without me. I continued to choke up privately as I penned these brief statements.

One sad evening, I scribbled a poem on a piece of yellow paper with a pencil that to this day I keep beside my bed. Through the window, I saw Deepa crying after a phone call with her friend. It was only March 25th, but it felt like I had been at MD Anderson for much, much longer.

To my dear wife...
My days are long
Mornings endless
Nights sleepless
I am sad, a bit shaken
I am sad, a bit broken
I feel the pain
I am hurting

I am shivering
I feel the sorrow
I am lonely as the walls close in
I feel the cage around me
I am living and dying
I have cancer in me
I see you, my dear
I see your face
I feel the sorrow in your eyes
I feel the tears rolling down
You are my angel; for you, I live

While on the isolation floor, I had two more bone marrow biopsies and many more CT scans. Thankfully, I was taken out of isolation for the scans, which offered a rare opportunity for Deepa and me to be together as I was transported to and back from the imaging center. This rare rendezvous would only last a few minutes but felt precious. She would be waiting outside the door and walk next to me. We secretly held our hands under the blankets.

I was scheduled to receive a third white blood cell transfusion during the first week of April. The whole time, I was unable to eat. I lost a lot of weight and looked different. I had dark spots on my face. They coalesced around my eyes and cast dark shadows. I lost all my facial hair. I saw my muscles waste away. I finally truly realized that I was in a serious fight for my life. I understood that these might be the last days of my humble existence.

But then again, I knew I had more life to live and more of myself to give. I knew that I was not finished yet. More importantly, I did not want to leave my wife. My son would survive; I knew that. He had already endured so much. But Deepa needed me. With that thought came my resolve to fight—fight for my life, my fight to keep my family intact.

Why Me?

Cancer raises many questions, though there are very few answers at hand. I struggled with questions as well, the most important being, "Why me?"

After much soul-searching, I finally realized that looking for an answer to this question is not helpful or productive. No one could answer that question—no textbook, friend, family member, or doctor.

Instead, I started asking, "Why not me?" What if this had happened to my wife or my son? If that had been the case, I might have wished it had happened to me instead. I found solace in the fact that I was at a point in my life where I could face this disease. I knew I had the fight in me.

Cancer is the ultimate test. It tests our logic, our reasoning, and our grit. It tries our relationships and forces change on our outlook on life. It's a cliche for a reason: facing death brings urgency to life.

The daily, intimate relationship with mortality can bring us to our very essence, our true selves. In doing so, cancer also brings clarity of thought and purity of mind. Cancer demands that you see what is important in life. It forces a reckoning with our life's purpose.

Once cancerous cells harbor within our bodies, we lose control of our lives. Cancer takes charge and takes over. It follows us everywhere, haunting and poking our softest places with its sharp, seemingly infinite tentacles. It is all-encompassing and furious, relentless in attack. We perceive it as a shameful disease that destroys our self worth. A label and a stigma that erodes hope and rots confidence. It clouds thoughts and plays games with minds. It tries to destroy the soul.

It truly is the emperor of all maladies.

It also defines us by how we cope with it. During my soul-searching, I wrote a poem on this very subject. I scribbled this sometime in the early days of my reckoning with cancer, though I forgot to put a date on it. By the time I wrote it, I had understood that there is never a good answer to the question "Why me?"

Why me?
Why me?
What did I do wrong?
What brought the curse upon me?
I search for answers
I search for the truth
None knew, and none could tell

It came to me then
Like a whisper
Like a soft blowing wind
Why not me?
Why not me?

My soul is pure
My mind is kind
I am strong
I have the fight in me
I have faith in me
I believe in angels now

My days will be longer,
My mornings meaningful

My nights filled with sleep
My days and nights will be mine
Not yours, cancer!

Soon, I would be facing the most difficult struggle of my life, crossing a new ocean filled with dangers. Still, I told myself to paddle and confront the deadly waves head-on. To make it to shore.

The Universe in Us

A well-known fact, though not often enough discussed in modern medicine: the ability to control one's thoughts can impact medical outcomes. Researchers have found that the genetic expression of various protein synthesis processes can be altered by only a few days of meditation or yoga. In the case of cancer, we can direct our bodies to produce more antibodies that will fight the disease. These can find and destroy cancerous cells.

Yes, there are a myriad of medications, piercing radiation, and radical surgeries. Targeted chemotherapy, modern cell therapy, gene therapy, and many other new therapies that are being discovered every day. But this is still a fight that one must delve into the soul to win, mustering all corners where courage and resolve reside in order to harness the fire within, the power of the inner soul. One must forge a connection with the true self. And make no mistake: the true self is incredibly powerful. In fact, one might say it has magic. The power of the self is the ultimate power.

Ironically, the unrelenting destruction of cancer ignites one's resolve to fight. This is the hardest war to undertake, replete with daily battles, including the most challenging: the ongoing clashes between self and self. (Here, I use all three terms interchangeably: inner soul, inner self, and true self.)

At the time of my diagnosis, I had no experience with meditation. Self-reflection, introspection, and soul-searching are foreign practices to many doctors. We are supposed to be strong and unwavering in times of crisis. As an interventional cardiologist, I was baptized by fire and had gotten used to death. But all this changed when I became the one walking in death's shadow.

It had been years since I'd thought of my grandmother reciting the Vedas—ancient scriptures dating back to 5000 BCE, containing mantras known to the ancient yogis of India designed to give the mind power to ward off death. But now they came back to me, clear as day. The *Maha Mrityunjay*, written in 1500 BCE, saved a powerful sage's son, who was destined to die at twelve. On his birthday, as foretold, the messenger of Death, Yama Raj, arrived to claim the boy. The boy, however, was determined to live, and he prayed to Lord Shiva, the most powerful creator, protector, and destroyer. In ancient Hindu mythology, Lord Shiva is seen as the soul of the Universe. Lord Shiva appeared from the sky and asked the boy to chant a mantra for a long life. The boy's repeated chanting warded off his untimely death.

The day I arrived at MD Anderson, a friend sent me a link to a video of the *Mrityunjay* mantra being chanted by priests. Many nights, I listened to it as I fell asleep, 3500 years after the mantra was written.

My friend Seema visited me the day after I arrived on the leukemia floor. She flew in from New Orleans as soon as she heard about my illness. I was not expecting her, and her arrival was a pleasant surprise. At the time, I was walking the corridors of the sixteenth floor to familiarize myself with its layout while clutching my portable IV pole.

Seema taught me a meditation that would help me find my true self as a modality for healing. She suggested I practice it daily and I did. I will forever be thankful for her kindness.

Another friend, Neelam, practices gastroenterology, and we have been friends for years. A Shiv Yogi—the belief in cosmic healing, in which individuals harness the power of the cosmos—she believes in and practices holistic medicine. When Neelam heard about my cancer, she reached out and told me that I should ask my body for more direct healing. She instructed me to write my specific healing targets on paper and then direct my body to act accordingly. She told me that many doctors are using this method in their healing journey. They believed that body-mind healing is an essential supplement to modern medical treatments.

It's also effective to tether healing targets in our mind—the ultimate canvas on which to create and visualize. It was entirely a new concept for me, but I had nothing to lose and took her advice. It worked wonders for me and helped me get through many crises. While in treatment, sometimes multiple times a day, I practiced this true-self meditation at home and in the hospital. I asked my body to accept the chemotherapy and heal by placing mental targets on my body to help direct my healing. These healing targets changed daily, and I wrote them down on paper to remind myself of them. I asked my body to focus on these targets. My nearby journal was opened multiple times a day. In it I recorded my hopes, fears, dreams, and prayers for myself, my family, and the world. I also listened to Vedic chants and gospel music. Meditation is a powerful tool to separate the mind from the pain in the body. I viewed my healing from a distance and envisioned myself as whole and healthy after my treatment.

These techniques of self-healing and meditation were foreign to me before my cancer diagnosis. They are simple yet powerful tools in fighting cancer or any other disease.

Recognizing and understanding our true selves takes practice, but once we unlock our souls and learn how to separate them from our minds, the harmony of our existence within the Universe becomes clear. All living and nonliving things are part of the larger Universe, a part of a harmonious webbed pattern that continuously dances like the ocean and coconut trees of my homeland.

In a peaceful setting, I would close my eyes and try to relax my body from head to toe. I preferred to do this while sitting up with a pillow behind my back, but on the days when I was weak, I did it lying down. Once comfortable and relaxed, I would begin meditation to bring myself to a state of tranquility and complete rest. This could take a few minutes.

I would close my eyes, focusing on my breathing for a few minutes until I was aware of nothing but my breath. I listened to my breath as it went in and out. It was the most soothing noise I had ever heard.

After a few minutes of this simple relaxation technique, I would move on to quieting my mind. This is easier than it sounds. Don't be intimidated. I will guide you through the process.

First, I stopped thinking about the past. Let go of it. The past is useless right now, anyway. It has no meaning or purpose in our current situations.

Next, stop thinking about the future. It is not important right now, either. Moreover, no one can predict it.

Just focus on the present. Keep awareness tuned into the breath. No thoughts, slow but steady, inhalation, exhalation.

Next, move the focus to the source of the breath. The seat of our lifeforce. Undefinable and indefinitely powerful.

I found that by holding two seemingly disparate truths in my heart simultaneously: surrender and targeted healing created a powerful paradox. I felt a sensation of glowing emptiness (surrender) while energy surged through me, healing the hotspots I'd directed it towards.

It is hard to define this formless presence, but we know it when we feel this true essence. The soul.

Breathing may naturally become faster, but I did my best to keep mine slow, deep, and steady. I felt a heaviness in my chest, a rush of emotions that I'd never experienced before.

For thousands of years, men and women have searched for the soul. Some have found it; some have not. Most never even tried, but it is always there, always available to us if we tune into this eternal flow of energy, our immortal souls.

Continue breathing gently and slowly open your eyes. Look around and thank the Universe for your life.

Each time I meditated, I stayed connected to this universal healing source and returned often. After a great deal of internet research and experimentation, I came to primarily depend on the true-self meditation taught by Moojiji called "An Invitation to Freedom." It is easily accessible on YouTube. I modified and added according to mood and what felt best. Each individual finds their way to the Universe through the portal of their own breathwork and our souls stretch to fill our bodies with healing light. All we have to do is tune in, stay in the moment, and request the most nourishing powers of the cosmos to sluice through us.

Before she left at the end of her first visit to the hospital, Seema offered me more wisdom as she turned around the corridor to the elevator. "Deepak, you will face tough and challenging moments in your battle with cancer. When faced with these adversities, I want you to be like a newborn in a cradle. Give yourself to the forces beyond your control. Offer yourself to the Universe unconditionally. Let the Universe heal and nurture you."

Then she turned the corner and returned to New Orleans.

Soul and Mind Check-In

Our mind and souls are two separate entities. We can dissociate our chattering minds, the culmination of our past thoughts and experiences, both good and bad, but not our pure souls. We cannot control our souls, we can only connect with them.

It is often said that controlling the mind is like trying to control the wind. Yet, the mind frequently strikes back, not wanting to be displaced as the director. When this occurs, we remind ourselves that our eternal soul is our true essence, and is not subject to being buffeted by the winds of change.

It is challenging, but becoming the wind in order to control the mind's negativity, helplessness, and despair is essential to recovery when tragedy strikes, and is one of the keys to happiness in day-to-day life. Dethroning the mind from its top dog spot reveals its tricks so it's easier not to fall for them. In the place of primacy, the soul can then direct our minds to hope and healing.

At the same time, true sadness is real and can weigh heavily on the heart. We cannot entirely ignore these emotions. Frequently "checking in" with the soul through regular meditation helps us overcome negativity and anger. I like to call it a "soul-and-mind check-in," since, once relegated to its proper place in the pecking order, our minds become instruments our soul can work with.

Our souls can only be intact and do not experience pain. One of the most powerful tools of my recovery was the reminder to myself: "Yes, I can take this pain. My mind is crying out, but my soul is not hurting."

The Science: Possibilities, Limits, and Decisions

I first met my transplant doctor—I will refer to her as Dr. Caring—in early March 2018. Dr. Caring's professional story was similar to mine—a doctor in a foreign country, she immigrated to the United States and retrained, adding a hematology-oncology fellowship followed by a year of stem cell transplantation training at MD Anderson, where she was employed as a full-time physician.

After one of my most difficult days in isolation, Dr. Caring came to my room late one evening. I couldn't clearly see her face as she wore a surgical mask. She told me that the leukemia team had recommended that I undergo a bone marrow transplant as a treatment.

Dr. Caring suggested that I check out the Center for International Blood and Marrow Transplant Research (CIBMTR) website, which details the state of transplantation in the United States. MD Anderson is a leader in this technology, performing around 800 marrow transplants a year.

There are two types of transplants. "Autologous" transplantation, transfuses a patient with their own previously harvested bone marrow. Usually the body can tolerate its own stem cells better than foreign cells. However, it can still fail, and some mortality is associated with the procedure. It also risks cancer returning, as some cancerous cells may lurk in the previously harvested bone marrow.

"Allogeneic" transplantation uses bone marrow from a different person. "Haploidentical transplantation" or "half-matched transplantation" is a transplant from a "related donor" who is the patient's child or parent. If the patient has an identical twin donor, it's a "syngeneic transplantation."

A donor not related to the patient, or "unrelated donor" includes cord blood transplantation, in which the transplanted stem cells are derived from umbilical cord blood. This is usually done as a last resort, though it is widely practiced. At the time of birth, the umbilical cord carries stem cells. However, the numbers are substantially lower than what can be extracted from a regular bone marrow transplant. These stem cells are then matched to the patient and transplanted. In these cases, the patient may need more than one cord blood transplant, or "double-cord blood transplantation."

In 2019, there were 14,000 autologous and 9,000 allogeneic transplantations. Approximately 60 percent of transplantations were autologous, and 40 percent were allogeneic. The number of transplants from sibling donors has slowly declined in the past few years, possibly due to smaller family sizes. At the same time, the number of transplants from parents or children is gradually increasing and has almost reached the number of transplants from siblings.

A patient's odds of surviving and reaching the five-year mark after transplantation depends on several factors. Most important is the type and nature of the disease. These transplants mainly treat cancers like multiple myeloma, lymphoma, and leukemia. Other conditions involving bone marrow dysfunction, like myelodysplastic syndrome, aplastic anemia, and sickle cell anemia are also treated with transplantation. They are rarely performed for autoimmune diseases. In children, syndromes involving congenital immunodeficiency are also treated with bone marrow transplantation.

With AML, the cancer I had, patients are classified as being in the low-, intermediate-, or advanced-risk categories. This is based on a risk score, which incorporates one's chromosomal and genetic characteristics.

In 2021, a person in the low-risk category had a 53% chance of crossing the five-year mark. For those in the intermediate-risk group—the group I belonged to—surviving past five years was literally 50/50.

These are depressing numbers, but a lot can change relatively quickly in cancer medicine.

AML is an uncommon cancer; still 20,000 patients in the United States will be diagnosed with AML, with a slight predominance in men and boys. Most pediatric leukemias are AML. Pediatric patients with AML have an excellent survival and cure rate.

The perseverance of Dr. Edward Thomas and his associates led to the successful transplantation procedure we know today. Born in 1920 near Waco, Texas, Thomas was the son of a country doctor. During his tenure at Harvard, he assisted a kidney transplant, and after graduating, he shifted to bone marrow transplantation.

The first reported case of bone marrow transplantation occurred in 1939 and was documented in the *Annals of Internal Medicine*. Unfortunately, the patient, a nineteen-year-old student, died a few weeks after undergoing this experimental therapy. In a landmark paper published in the *New England Journal of Medicine* on September 12th, 1957, Dr. Thomas and colleagues reported the results of bone marrow infusions in six patients who had undergone radiation and chemotherapy prior to the transplant. All six patients lived for some time; however, they died within one hundred days. This represented a major achievement compared to previous treatments, which only extended a patient's life by a few weeks.

Over the next few decades, Dr. Thomas continued to study and refine the process of stem cell transplantation. By 1979, he had achieved excellent survival rates, and these patients were free of their disease in the near term.

Dr. Thomas retired in 1990, the same year he was awarded the Nobel Prize in Medicine for advancing the field of bone marrow transplantation.

Bone marrow or stem cell transplantation is an evolving field. We are just scratching the surface of this lifesaving therapy. Sadly, it remains prohibitively expensive for many, and access is limited in less prosperous countries. There are far too many post-transplantation side effects, and they are not well understood. The procedure still carries a high mortality risk, especially true when it comes to transplantation from unrelated donors.

The side effects of bone marrow transplantation are incredibly taxing on the body as well as on the spirit. These side effects depend upon the type of transplantation one receives and the intensity of the chemotherapy beforehand. Autologous transplantations are far less dramatic or painful. In unrelated transplants, side effects are more common. One common side effect is severe ulcers in the mouth and mucous membranes, which invariably lead to difficulty eating and drinking. This results in profound weight loss. Serious infections, skin burns, and outright rejection of the transplant can also occur.

Another dreaded complication is Graft Versus Host Disease (GVHD), which occurs when new blood cells produced by the donor marrow view the host's body as foreign and attack the organs of their new body. This can happen immediately after the transplant procedure or be delayed. The condition, which can be life-threatening, can continue for months or even years. These reactions must be treated with high doses of steroids and other very potent immunosuppressive medications. GVHD can still occur despite the careful matching process between host and donor. The pain and discomfort in the days after transplantation can be so significant that many patients end up on morphine pumps for days at a time. There is a high likelihood of losing significant muscle mass to the point where the patient needs assistance with daily activities and basic movement.

With this comes substantial psychological trauma, depression, and anxiety. After the procedure, patients must stay close to the transplant center—within a thirty-minute drive—for the first ninety days. During these first ninety days, patients travel back and forth for frequent checkups, usually stressful, and often include complications that necessitate re-admission to the hospital.

It takes an army to care for a stem cell transplant patient. There are whole floors dedicated to this procedure, with highly specialized transplant doctors and nurses, physiotherapists, occupational therapists, social workers, and clergy.

Before the transplant, patients and their families are counseled about the difficulties they will invariably face during this process. The necessary long absence from work can lead to serious financial challenges for patients undergoing transplantation, which can cause severe stress and psychological problems, including depression, anxiety, and post-traumatic stress disorder (PTSD). It tests the endurance of even the most physically and mentally fit.

My choices in terms of my bone marrow transplant were starkly different and far from clear. The current science fell short when the path diverged in front of me. Opinions from experts in the field were as different as day and night.

The Search for a Donor

The logical place to begin to look for a donor was with my siblings, starting with my identical twin. All my siblings live in India except my twin, who had settled in Kuala Lumpur. MD Anderson handled the matching process. They sent testing kits to India and Kuala Lumpur. There was some difficulty in sending the samples back, however, as there are certain restrictions on transporting human samples. Courier companies were initially unwilling to transport blood or mouth swabs. Luckily, we were able to overcome these difficulties to undergo the matching process.

Matching for stem cell or bone marrow transplantation is called human leukocyte antigen (HLA) typing. It is a complex process involving multiple steps. A living cell has a certain number of protein-based structures on its outer layer that are like spikes—the HLA markers. There are three main groups of HLA markers: A, B, and DR. Each contains many subgroups. We inherit these HLA proteins from our parents, hence the greater likelihood of siblings being a match. The more siblings one has, the more chances of finding a close match.

Seven out of ten patients looking for a sibling match end up with a "mismatch"—HLA proteins in the patient's cells not aligning with those of a potential donor's.

In my case, none of my siblings in India were a match, but my identical twin brother was, as expected, a full match. However, I learned that accepting a transplant from an identical twin carries a much higher chance of the disease returning, the dreaded "relapse." There have been many cases of leukemia occurring in identical twins, sometimes separated only by a span of months. When a patient accepts marrow from an identical twin, the graft-versus-tumor effect—defined as new bone-marrow-producing cells identifying and killing the leukemic cells—often fails because the twin's marrow is too similar and can't read the cancer cells as dangerous.

The transplant community has no unified recommendation on these so-called "syngeneic transplants," in part because these transplants are rare. First, one must be diagnosed with a condition that requires stem cell transplantation. Add to that the unlikelihood of having an identical twin, and you can see how uncommon my situation was.

Deepa and I struggled with what we should do. On the one hand, I had a full match with my twin brother, yet receiving a transplant from him carried significant risks. On the other hand, we didn't know whether I would find any non-related matches in the United States.

In the United States, only about 25 percent of patients looking for a match find one in a sibling. The other 75 percent must look for a non-related match. When that happens, they are directed to nonprofit transplant registries. The National Marrow Donor Program (NMDP) is the largest and most important donor registry in the United States, with over nineteen million individuals and growing by the day. Transplant programs work with NMDP to find matches for their patients. They also store umbilical cord blood for those who do not find a suitable donor. In addition, NMDP works with international donor programs in Europe and elsewhere and has over forty million strong databases of potential donors.

Currently, over half of transplants in the United States arranged through NMDP involve foreign donors.

This is where humanity wins through love and sacrifice. A donor has no religion or political affiliation. Race and gender don't show up in this life-preserving, selfless act. A trip to the doors of death reminds us that we all belong to one another, branches of a common tree. The human tree.

Finding a non-related match is difficult because HLA antigens have evolved over the centuries. When all the genetic variations are taken together, there are about ten billion possible HLA variations. The odds of having a similar HLA in two unrelated persons are less than one in twenty thousand.

People of African descent have lived on this planet the longest and have undergone various intermixing involving different ethnic groups. Hence, their gene pool is diverse and complex, making it difficult to find a match. Due to the complexity of the gene pools, patients of mixed race have the most difficulty finding a match. Caucasian patients currently have the best chance, with two out of three finding a match. In the United States, Asians, Hispanics, and African Americans find it much harder to find a suitable match. In this situation, being diverse can be a curse. The chances of a nonwhite person in the United States finding a match falls between 20 and 40%.

In my case, the NMDP database had less than a million participants of Asian descent at the time of my cancer. These then broke down into subgroups of Indian, Korean, Filipino, Chinese, Vietnamese, and Japanese origin. There were around 250,000 potential donors of South Asian or Indian origin.

We spent days and weeks trying to decide what to do. Everyone had a different opinion about receiving a transplant from your twin. Overwhelmingly, the opinions were against accepting it.

It was an agonizing time waiting for a reply from the registry. I was also undergoing chemotherapy during this period.

Then came the surprise of our lives.

In my next follow-up meeting with Dr. Caring, she informed us that I had hundreds of full matches in the registry. This was a total surprise and a turning point in my journey. That said, accepting a non-related donor—even if they were a full match—could still be difficult. The transplant process itself would be harder than with a transplant from my twin brother, with an increased risk of complications.

On top of everything, the potential donor had to be in good health and must go through an additional screening process to rule out the possibility of having hepatitis, HIV, or some other communicable disease. Ideally, a donor should be less than forty years-old and willing to go through the stem cell donation process.

Fortunately, the majority of patients who donate bone marrow do not have to undergo any surgical procedure to collect the marrow. Most adults who donate bone marrow are given daily injections of a bone marrow stimulant for a few days on an outpatient basis. Then, on the fourth or fifth day, they go to a blood bank or collection center and have their blood drawn. There, the blood passes through a cell separator, and the bone marrow cells are separated. The rest of the blood is then automatically routed back into the body. This process takes a few hours. It is not laborious, but it is time-consuming. There is also some discomfort involved for the donor due to the increased production of bone marrow cells, which causes pain. There is also the issue of the required time off from work or school. Matched donors may have life circumstances that would prevent donation. They may even be out of town or out of the country. So, having a potential match—or matches—does not guarantee that one will receive a donation. In fact, it is quite common to *not* get a donation, even with a potential match in the registry.

As we grappled with the implications of going this route, we were informed that the committee overseeing MD Anderson's transplantation had decided that I ought to accept my twin brother's marrow.

MD Anderson Cancer Center is a world leader in stem cell transplantation, also called bone marrow transplantation or hematopoietic cell transplantation. However, this decision contradicted what my leukemia team believed was best. I requested a meeting with the head of MD Anderson's transplantation services.

Dr. Caring was present for this meeting, as were Soorya and Deepa. The senior doctor acknowledged that there was a higher risk of relapse if I went with a donation from my twin. Still, he suggested that I accept his donation. If and when I relapsed, I could then try an unrelated match. He focused on the ease of the process and the smooth recovery if I went with my twin versus a difficult and complicated recovery with an unrelated donor.

Hearing this, I glanced over at Deepa. Her eyes were wide with fear. Soorya asked questions, wanting to know more, though I do not recall what he asked. I, too, asked questions and brought up the issue of relapse. The professor left the room, leaving us with Dr. Caring.

If we went this route, the constant fear of relapse would be like living with a Sword of Damocles hanging over me. According to the data, if I used my twin's donation, I'd be living with 50% chance of relapse within three years compared to a 16% chance of relapse when the transplant comes from an unrelated donor.

I was at a crossroads, needing to make a choice.

Crossroads

Intersections occur throughout our lives. Some represent minor choices; others are critically important. When we take the road less traveled, the outcomes are less predictable. While forging a newer path or making an unconventional choice is touted as being wholly positive, the risks are great. Robert Frost wrote "The Road Not Taken" to lightly mock a good friend's indecisiveness about the men's walks in the woods. But the friend, Edward Thomas, took it more seriously and joined the British army in 1915, even though, as a father of three and in his thirties, he was excused from serving. He was killed in action in 1917.

Deepa's intuition cautioned against me receiving the transplant from my brother. I trusted my wife with my life. Her clarity of her decision was a pointer I needed to heed.

I could not imagine going through this dreaded cancer again. Another rendezvous with AML would certainly result in me giving up entirely. Plus, the general assumption in the cancer world is that outcomes tend to be poorer with each relapse. I think bone marrow transplantation from an identical twin should be limited to situations where no other suitable matches are available. There is understandably a lack of consensus on this in the medical community. My own leukemia doctor advised against receiving a donation from my twin at the outset. Dr. Caring also had reservations about it from the beginning. We were dealing with a rare clinical situation, and opinions differed because the available scientific opinion and the data were limited and outdated.

A decision was then made to take the difficult route and go against the committee's recommendation—"the one less traveled by," as Frost wrote. And looking back, yes, it "has made all the difference."

We made the decision then and there and conveyed it to Dr. Caring. Once I explained the medical details behind the decision to my twin, he agreed and was relieved. My family and I were happy with our choice, though we knew the road before us would be hard.

Like the British poet, I chose the road that needed the fight.

Once the decision was made, the transplant coordinator got to work. It took less than a month to set a date for my transplant. In transplantation circles, this is called our new birthday. It is a new beginning, a fresh start to life.

The Calm Before the Storm: Waiting for the Transplant

April 5, 2018, MD Anderson, Houston

I remained in isolation for just over a month. By the end of that period, my white blood cell count had returned to near normal. My second bone marrow biopsy completed while I was in isolation confirmed that my leukemia was in remission.

By now, I had completed four bone marrow biopsies.

The doctors slowly weaned me off intravenous antibiotics as my white cell count returned to near normal. I was discharged from the hospital. As I packed my belongings, I caught a glimpse of myself in the mirror. I looked different. My facial hair had almost disappeared, my skin had darkened, and dark circles framed my eyes. I had lost a significant amount of weight.

The nurses applauded as we left the isolation floor.

Deepa and I held hands as we walked out of the hospital together into the open and free world. It was April 5, Texas spring in full color. In the garden next to the emergency room the roses were in full bloom and a light morning breeze caressed my darkened cheeks.

The freedom from isolation felt magical. We took pictures together and sent them to our friends.

My cancer journey was not over, however. This was just the first act. I still had a number of treatments ahead of me, so we were not cleared to return home to Baton Rouge. Instead, we checked into Rotary House next door.

The next act in my performance would prove to be a real-life drama filled with suspense, months of despair, and days when I wished my suffering would end. I was at peace with any outcome.

Healing from Within

Harnessing the body-mind healing interaction complements modern medicine. After all, modern medicine does have limitations in its current form, especially when it comes to cancer treatment. It acts as a destroyer aimed at obliterating cancer cells. But in doing so, it also kills healthy living and reproducing cells. In addition, more direct chemotherapy, called targeted chemotherapy, is only available for a few types of cancer.

Healing in its purest form means that the patient ultimately returns to a state of wholeness. This involves regenerating all healthy original tissues and cells. This is where the body-mind connection comes in.

At Neelam's direction, I started utilizing body-mind interaction early in my chemotherapy. I asked my body for various favors. I asked my bone marrow to produce more platelets, white blood cells, and hemoglobin. I asked my body to work with the medicines and not fight them. I asked my body to accept the chemotherapy and not react negatively. Later in my treatment, I asked my newborn cells to stop attacking my body. I asked for my fever to stop and my vertigo to go away. I asked for less pain and more sleep. My requests to my body varied daily or weekly, depending on the situation. And despite going through multiple rounds of chemotherapy lasting weeks at a time, I never had a severe or adverse reaction to a chemotherapeutic agent. This is critical because, in cancer medicine, the ability to tolerate chemotherapy can mean the difference between life and death. With each round of chemotherapy, I gently asked my body to accept the medicines and transfusions without causing any severe adverse reactions. Later, when I had a bone marrow transplant, I asked my body to accept the transplant.

One can improve our chances of beating cancer by harnessing the power of our inner self, enabling the body-mind connection to work at its fullest, and allowing the Universe to aid in healing. The more we practice body-mind healing, the more revealing that the true power of healing lies within us.

What we are looking for is already within us. We are our own ultimate healers.

Consolidation Treatment

After that day of freedom and applause, I was readmitted to MD Anderson on the 9th of April. As such, I would have to undergo a number of treatments, including additional chemotherapy, called consolidation therapy, to keep me cancer-free while I waited for my team to find a match.

The medications I received in this round of chemotherapy were similar to those in my first intensive chemotherapy treatment. The main difference was that this round lasted fewer days and was tailored to my current blood cell counts.

I returned to the hospital again, from May 7th to May 9th, for additional consolidation chemotherapy. Between these hospital stays, I had multiple outpatient visits and needed frequent blood transfusions and swallowed handfuls of prophylaxis medications designed to prevent infections and shingles. Through it all, I met with transplant doctors, nurses, coordinators, and social workers to prepare for the transplant day, circling closer every hour. My salvation, or so I prayed.

A Fateful Call

Intermission was over.

It all happened fast. My transplant coordinator called me at the beginning of June. We waited for this call every day and night in April and May. Then, just like that, the call came. We were driving when she called. Deepa pulled over to the VA Medical Center parking lot. The coordinator was excited. I took my paper and pen, which I carried with me everywhere, expecting this call. She had a donor and arranged a date for the transplant. She asked me to get ready to be hospitalized a week before the transplantation. She gave us the instructions and the dates. We looked at each other in disbelief as I wrote down the instructions word by word. We sat in the car for a long time trying to process the news and thinking about the next phase in our lives. We were excited but also scared of the unknown. They had warned me about the potential to lose my life with this treatment. One in five patients could die from complications related to bone marrow transplantation. Yet, finally, it was happening.

We wondered who the donor was. Little did we know that the donor would become a part of our family and life in two years, bringing us and the scientific community even more surprises.

The transplant coordinator was unable to disclose that information.

I had to undergo a "conditioning regimen," a highly aggressive regimen of chemotherapy to set the stage for the bone marrow transplant. My transplant date was set for Wednesday, June 20, 2018.

On Wednesday, June 13, 2018, we checked in after five in the evening when my bed became available on the seventeenth floor. Soon, every inch of my body, including my privates, was examined and documented in considerable detail. This ritual was conducted with two nurses in attendance. They took pictures with a digital camera, which were then uploaded to my medical records. I would stay there for one month and be discharged on July 12th.

It was the most difficult and heartbreaking month of my life.

I am forever changed.

Day of Transplantation: A New Beginning

My transplant was scheduled for approximately three months after my team made the decision, which is considered a good turnaround time in the world of transplantation. It could very well take much longer to find a match and then receive the transplant. After the delays that pushed my procedure back from June 20th to June 21st, everything seemed to be on track.

I woke up on Thursday, June 21, 2018, my body thrumming with nerves.

My room had an unobstructed view of Hermann Park. A hot, cloudless day, the trees outside my window sagged in the heat.

Deepa was already up and praying. Soorya had come in from the Caribbean. He had a cold and a sore throat and was not allowed in the room due to the risk of transmitting the illness to me. He peeped in through the doors instead.

My room was right across from the nurses' station. I heard chatting in multiple languages. The cacophony was comforting.

My nurse, Abby, had been with me during the day shift the last few days. She was a very competent and caring nurse with many years of experience, but she was nervous about my transplant scheduled for today after a delay due to bad weather. Transported by commercial carrier, the marrow would be accompanied by a volunteer transporter, who ensures the transplant is handed over to the medical center staff. The MD Anderson staff would collect the transplant from the airport and transport it safely to the Cancer Center, at least an hour drive. There was suspense in the air, not knowing whether the transplant would arrive on time.

At 9:30, Abby informed us that the transplant had arrived. It was delivered to my floor by 10:30 in the morning. It looked just like a regular blood transfusion bag with labels on it. The color was somewhat different from that of normal blood, though. The stem cells added a peachy-orange color to the bag. These were the living cells of a completely unrelated person. We are, and will always be, deeply thankful for that selfless soul.

At 11:00 a.m., Abby went through the usual cross-checking process with the other nurses and me—a meticulous process undertaken before any blood transfusion. The labels on the back of the bag are read aloud, the recipient's name is read aloud, and two nurses and the patient confirm the match. The attending doctor making the rounds gave the official go-ahead.

The transfusion started at 11:06 a.m. on Thursday, June 21, 2018— my new birthday. Soorya looked through the open doors. Deepa, next to me, prayed with her beads, eyes closed. Abby stayed with me, a broad smile on her face. I watched the flow of stem cells into my body—a slow drip of new cells that could save my life. I prayed for a good outcome and asked my body not to react to the transfusion.

The transfusion lasted an hour and I did well. My transplant was now inside me, witnessed by my wife and son. My new lease to play out the second act of my life had been given to me by a stranger unknown to us. All we knew was that my donor was a twenty-four-year-old male who had the same blood group as me. It was the gift of life. Part of him would live within me for the rest of my life. This unknown man's marrow cells would now make their home in me. Within weeks, they would start producing healthy cells. My marrow had been wiped away by intense chemotherapy before this. The treatment regimen I received had been toxic and painful. Now, it was time for my body to accept my new marrow. I prayed that it would. I prayed for a smooth post-transplantation experience. However, I knew that my road to recovery would be painful, with months and possibly years of difficulties ahead.

Once the transfusion was complete, Abby stepped out of the room. Just as she left, I started experiencing chills. It was an allergic reaction to the transplant. Abby immediately ran back in and gave me prednisone and antihistamines. The reaction slowly subsided.

The excitement wore off as the realities of post-transplant life revealed themselves. The cruelty of cancer was on full display. It was the start of months of agony. I lost track of time. These dark days have scarred me forever.

Post-Transplant Days: Caught in a Ferocious Storm

Over the next few days, weeks, and months, I was a textbook example of all that can go wrong with stem cell transplantation. Everything that could have gone wrong did . . . except for the fact that it did not take me with it. Everything except my soul was crushed.

The day after the transplantation, I was diagnosed with bilateral pneumonia. Doctors had to keep changing antibiotics.

By June 24th, my skin started to burn and peel. My private areas felt as if a bomb had exploded down there, complete with burned, scalded skin. Both sides of my hands developed significant blisters, as did both feet. Nurses worked tirelessly to dress these areas and apply various creams and lotions. My mouth and gastrointestinal tract also burned up and blistered, a condition called mucositis. I could not eat or drink for weeks at a time. Even swallowing my saliva caused intense pain.

At first, the transplant team wasn't sure why I was developing these large blisters on my palms and soles. Soon, it was clear that they resulted from the dreaded acute GVHD. Any little movement caused intense pain as the skin around my privates and on my armpits was stripped away. I was put on multiple antibiotics and antifungals to prevent infection.

On June 24th, I was connected to a morphine pump. This pump

stayed with me for days and was only disconnected on July 2nd. They kept increasing my morphine dosage so I could get some relief from my pain and suffering. I consider myself to have high pain tolerance, so I was not happy to be on morphine or any other opiate. Morphine made me feel like one of the living dead. I would sleep for hours at a time, then wake up briefly, only to go back to sleep again. I once slept for nearly forty-eight hours straight. Deepa was scared by how I looked and acted. My days and nights got messed up. I lost track of time. My senses were blurred. Every act of my living, except breathing, caused intense pain. My blood count hit rock bottom, and I needed multiple blood transfusions. I was constantly nauseous and stopped eating and drinking. I tried to suck on ice, but even that was too painful.

I looked and acted like a confused, helpless ghost in intolerable pain and suffering, wanting to escape this world. Nurses and doctors looked at me with sadness and anxiety on their faces. They were doing everything they could. They were worried for me. Deepa was distraught. In shock, no more tears left, isolated from her friends and family, watching me slip by. My weight plummeted to the point that they were thinking of tube feeding.

On the night of the 27th, I started having difficulty breathing. I couldn't lie flat and had to sit up to catch my breath. I started sweating profusely. My heart rate shot up, and I needed oxygen to keep my blood oxygen saturation up. Seeing my distress, Deepa called the nurse. She, in turn, called the nurse practitioner covering the floor. It was midnight by then. The floor was silent except for the movement of medication trays and the cries of an elderly patient who appeared to curse in Arabic. He was in the next room and had the transplant before me. His wife was trying to console and comfort him.

The nurse practitioner examined me and ordered a series of tests, including an ECG and an X-ray. I asked whether she could check for BNP, an indicator of heart failure, to which she obliged. I knew what was happening to me. It is called acute pulmonary edema, and I have seen it hundreds of times. This generally occurs when you receive an overload of fluids. This can include antibiotics, chemotherapy, and transfusions. The overload causes fluid to build up in the lungs, and if not treated promptly, it can become serious and life-threatening.

I tried to communicate this with the night staff and the nurse practitioner and politely asked for Lasix, the immediate treatment. I knew that a chest X-ray could look like pneumonia and might be confusing to even experienced eyes. However, I had trouble communicating my expertise and spent most of the night sitting up in bed, breathing hard. Finally, I was given Lasix, and I soon felt better. The next day, during rounds, my attending physician confirmed that it was indeed acute pulmonary edema caused by fluid overload. Since this incident, the staff has routinely sought the help of cardiologists.

My engraftment began on July 1, 2018; my marrow started producing cells. It had been twelve days since the transplant, but it felt like an eternity. While one might think this would be cause for celebration, it was the most difficult period of my life. During those endless days and nights, I saw the cruelty of cancer. It almost wholly crushed my soul. There were moments when I wished for my suffering to end, and it did not matter how. For the first time, I understood how one could welcome the end and be at peace with it.

I also felt like a baby in the cradle, powerless and expecting the Universe to heal me. I surrendered myself to the divine, to heal me, not knowing the outcome, at peace with the possibility of living or dying. Once I relinquished control, I experienced an incredible sense of calm and peace, one of the most miraculous feelings one can encounter.

I was unbelievably weak. For the first time since I was an infant, I could not walk. I had to move around in a wheelchair and needed help with almost everything. I lost about forty pounds in six weeks, a significant portion of my body weight.

The opiates were gradually weaned off as I hated how they made me feel. I returned to the mechanism to deal with the pain I had practiced while in isolation: I meditated and separated my soul from my body. By this point, I had learned to direct my body to tolerate the pain. I dug deep into my soul when the agony seemed almost too much to endure. I separated my body and soul and continuously reminded myself that my soul was intact and that only my body was hurting. I also kept telling myself that I could handle this pain. I did the same thing every time I received bad news. This became my primary coping mechanism. It was a respite from the trauma and assault on my body and mind.

Human beings are not designed to withstand long periods of pain and misery. It is unnatural for us. Even worse, we are never taught how to deal with such shocks to our systems, whether it be in the form of a tragic loss, such as the death of an immediate family member, or a serious sickness visiting us, like cancer. Different people have different escape and coping mechanisms. When we emerge from these unnatural experiences, our minds will be different. They are and will be permanently traumatized and scarred. No matter how we handle it, these traumatic experiences will always leave serious marks on our souls and bodies.

During this treatment and recovery period, immediate family members were allowed to stay with patients, so Deepa stayed by my side the whole time. However, visitation by family and friends is generally discouraged on the transplant floor due to the risk of them carrying illness or infection. Children are not allowed at all. As a result, I had only a few visitors except Donna, who visited often and stayed in Houston as much as she could. These visits brought us some degree of normalcy.

I stayed in the hospital for four weeks. On July 12th, I was well enough to be released with help and supervision. I appreciated everything that had been done for me. There was some anxiety within me about the discharge and whether I would be able to cope at the apartment, but the joy of going home soon overtook all those feelings. I needed a wheelchair for transportation, though at home, I could walk with assistance. The blisters on my hands and feet were still very much present and painful.

I tried never to be a difficult patient. Over the years, I had heard countless stories about how doctors make terrible patients, and I didn't want to become another such story. I hoped I was successful because my nurses seemed to love working with and caring for me. They all loved Deepa and brought her home-cooked food.

Discharged, I was required to stay close to MD Anderson for at least three months. After I was released, Deepa and I returned to the one-bedroom apartment we rented near the hospital, just a five-minute drive away. It was across the street from Hermann Park, which I had seen from my room on the seventeenth floor of the Cancer Center. The park is a respite for many patients and their families, and it serves many hospitals in the area, with multiple entrances. Deepa and I spent many evenings enjoying the breeze in the park and watching the day pass into the night.

I was told that many of my patients and staff back in Zachary prayed for me daily. They had prayer meetings at the office and in the nearby churches. These prayer meetings had taken place every week since I first got sick. Deepa and I received countless letters offering support and prayers. Prayer books, prayer mats, and various religious ornaments came in through the mail. The support was overwhelming, and I will forever be thankful for it. Through this experience, Deepa and I realized the immense importance of human support and interaction in the healing process.

It was wise to be ordered to remain close to the hospital. In the short time that had elapsed from my discharge day, I had been hospitalized twice for GVHD. Both times, I stayed in the hospital for days at a time.

The first hospitalization was on July 24th, just twelve days after my discharge from the transplantation floor. After my discharge, I could not eat or drink for days. I vomited frequently and had intense abdominal pain. I could not sleep due to the pain. I didn't want to return to the hospital and decided to wait, hoping it would just go away with time. However, I grew sicker and sicker and finally asked Deepa to take me back to the hospital. I was admitted immediately with dehydration. My bowels were not working. I was put on a high dose of intravenous steroids, fluids, and various other medicines. Dr. Caring ordered an endoscopy to examine my digestive tract. They found severe GVHD in my gastrointestinal tract, including my stomach, bowels, and rectum. I also had an ulcer in my esophagus. This was a serious problem that could potentially lead to my death.

Dr. Caring was deeply concerned. I could see it in her eyes. She told me, "You have grade-four GVHD. We're going to take it slowly and carefully." Grade-four GVHD is the worst form of this complication and could be potentially fatal. It carries a very high mortality rate. These could be my last few days or weeks on earth.

I stayed in the hospital until August 4th and was discharged with a prescription for a high dose of oral prednisone, a steroid used to treat inflammation. By then, I could eat and drink again, but I still had blisters on my palms and soles. My muscles were weak. The steroids made me feel like a zombie. I was agitated and sleepless. On a good night, I was able to sleep for two or three hours. My blood sugar climbed so high that I was put on insulin and other diabetic medicines. I lost my sense of smell and taste; everything tasted like cardboard. I received medication infusions at home. Physical and occupational therapists also visited me at home.

My second hospitalization began two weeks after I was discharged again. On August 17th, I was readmitted for another GVHD flare-up. My medications were increased, and I started taking more potent immunosuppressants called secondary agents. I stayed in the hospital until August 21st and was then discharged.

During this admission, I developed another dreaded effect of transplantation: the reactivation of viral infections. Everyone has viruses present in their bodies, usually from childhood infection. In a healthy person, these viruses remain dormant. However, when the immune system is weak, they reactivate and wreak havoc. They are also potentially lethal.

I had two viruses reactivated. One was called cytomegalovirus, and the other was called BK virus. The cytomegalovirus can infect multiple organs and cause serious damage or even death. However, in my experience, the BK virus was the more dreadful of the two. It infected my bladder and caused me immense difficulty for weeks. It caused severe burning during urination and felt like a constant fire in my bladder. My urine became red, and I passed blood clots. The urge to urinate was relentless. Those were difficult days and weeks in which I felt terrible and down. There was nothing to look forward to except painful days and sleepless nights.

Throughout all this, my GVHD was relentless. Large indwelling catheters were inserted in my body, which made it easier to receive medicines and transfusions. The nurses could also do blood draws through them. These catheters stayed in for months, almost like an additional organ. They became an extension of my body. I had to care for and clean them with a special routine to keep the area around them from becoming infected.

My doctors were concerned about me throughout this period. I could see it in their eyes.

As a physician, I often wanted to research my disease and its management. At first, I did research using the resources I had. At some point, though, I realized that this was counterproductive. Everything I read increasingly led me to a place of darkness, worry, and uncertainty. I stopped researching my disease and its treatment, choosing to let the professionals take care of me. Deepa also refused to research my condition and its outcomes. She believed in the system and felt her uncompromising faith would carry me through this dreaded disease.

For many months after my transplant, time had no meaning to me. Days became months. My treatment dominated every aspect of my life. I had to be incredibly careful to avoid infections, as I was on high doses of immunosuppressant medications. I was also on anti-rejection medications. I had severe muscle weakness due to high doses of steroids, coupled with muscle loss and wasting. Deepa wheeled me around in a wheelchair. Her legs became mine for weeks. She took over all aspects of my life, from bathing to feeding and comforting.

I had to learn how to walk again with physiotherapy. The hardest thing was climbing stairs or walking on an incline. It felt surreal to take baby steps with a physiotherapist.

Even after I was discharged, I visited the hospital almost daily. We had a routine for these visits. Deepa would drive me to the hospital and drop off the car with the valet service at MD Anderson. This is a convenient service for patients that allows you to get out right at the hospital entrance. We would then get a wheelchair at the hospital entrance to navigate through the clinics and testing. Once the day's treatment ended, Deepa would get the car from the valet and drive me back home. In time, we became friends with many people at the valet service, the infusion center, and the laboratory.

The summer of 2018 was hot and relentless, with hardly any rain. I can count the days that it rained on my fingers. I have never been exposed to such intense heat in my life, even though I am from southern India. We had plenty of rain in India, which cooled the air. Louisiana also has its fair share of rain. Houston's summer was different--the air was humid, and it stayed hot all day and night. The heat made my daily commute to the hospital difficult.

Just like in New York, life never stops in Houston. I watched the rhythm of the city from my balcony all summer long. My apartment overlooked Interstate 288, and I had a clear view of downtown. I had a front-row seat to the dramas of life, with nothing but time to watch.

Some weekends, Deepa drove me to the beach about forty-five minutes south of the Cancer Center. We sat by the beach and caught the wind coming off the water. We watched the birds and the ships pass by. We enjoyed the evening sun. These evenings took me back to my childhood.

One evening, I got out of the car and walked onto the sandy beach, even though I was not allowed to walk on the sand due to the risk of infection. I had to touch the water. Soon, the waves were caressing my legs. The wind spoke to me gently. I stood knee-deep in the water for several minutes and watched the sunset and the clouds pass overhead. There were ships in the distance. Deepa left her worry in the car and joined me. We held hands as if we had just met. We enjoyed this moment of bliss, of normalcy. I didn't want it to end.

The Passing of the Storm

All bad things must eventually pass. There will be a new day, a new dawn. In my case, we longed for the good days to return, and they did, slowly but surely. I began to improve. My blood count got better and my strength slowly returned. By late October, we were making plans to go back to Baton Rouge. It has been eight long months since that fateful Monday in February when my world changed. Winter had given way to a long, relentless Texas summer, and now it was fall. Just as the seasons changed, my life changed, too.

I would still need regular doctor's visits and continuous treatment, but this could be done at Ochsner Medical Center in New Orleans. They also have a stem cell transplant program. Mike Castine, my hematologist back home, had already spoken with them and arranged for my visits.

We vacated our apartment in Houston on October 25th and drove home. The drive back to Louisiana was emotional. We departed Houston around noon to beat the traffic and reached home by early evening. We didn't stop anywhere on the highway.

Back home, frail after losing so much muscle mass and on multiple medications, it was essential I continue following serious infection prevention protocols. But I was home, and home felt like heaven.

I read a lot and watched TV. I visited Mike at his office and made trips to Ochsner for checkups. I wore a mask outdoors.

About a month later, we celebrated Thanksgiving at home in Baton Rouge with Soorya. We had so much to be thankful for.

Deepa made preparations for a Hindu religious practice called *mundan* to pray for my continued recovery. It involves ritually shaving one's head in a temple with the help of a priest. It cannot be done in just any Hindu temple around the world, only in the temple in the city of Tirupati, in the state of Andhra Pradesh, where a deity accepts the ritually shaved hair as an offering. She would have to travel to India.

Naturally blessed with a full head of curly hair that she had difficulty straightening and containing, I couldn't imagine my wife without her lustrous mane. I tried to dissuade her, but she was committed to making this sacrifice.

Due to transportation issues, Deepa was unable to reach Tirupati. But her sister took her to a temple in Chennai, in Tamil Nadu, where *mundan* is also practiced. There, she performed the *mundan* ceremony, asking God for my full recovery.

Deepa stayed with her sister and mother during this visit. Her father had passed away many years earlier due to a heart attack. For the first time, she revealed my cancer diagnosis to her mother.

Seeing pictures of Deepa with no hair brought me to tears. Soorya, who was staying with me while she was away, consoled me. It was true that Deepa looked beautiful and divine, even without hair. Possibly more so. She assured me that she felt peaceful and had no hesitation. "This is the least I could do for you," she said. "I would do it for you again."

While Deepa was in India, GVHD reared its painful head. I returned to Houston with Soorya to see Dr. Caring, who put me on high-dose steroids again. She was concerned and recommended that I undergo Extracorporeal Photopheresis (ECP).

She arranged for this while I was still in Houston. This treatment, which lasted several months, is for patients with difficult-to-treat GVHD and is only offered in specialized centers. For up to three hours, I would be connected to an ECP machine, which exposed my blood to ultraviolet radiation to tame my white blood cells. I needed to have a large catheter inserted. A vascular surgeon did this while I was under anesthesia. This catheter, which was the size of my middle finger, caused me a great deal of discomfort and stayed with me until late March of the following year. This was the last-ditch effort to beat GVHD.

Hearing this news, Deepa returned to the United States sooner than expected. Soorya and I met her at Houston International Airport. It was close to midnight when her flight arrived, and a surprising number of Buddhist monks were in the airport that evening. I suspected that they had also been on Deepa's flight. The monks practice *mundan*, or head-shaving, throughout their lives. Seeing them brought me a feeling of serenity and calmness.

Seeing Deepa, I kissed her bald head. The three of us hugged for a long time.

I did my initial ECP sessions at MD Anderson. Once back in Baton Rouge, I continued the ECP treatment at Ochsner in New Orleans. I also had regular appointments with Mike Castine, my hematologist, in town.

By January, almost a year after the muscle pain in my office, I felt well enough to return to work on a part-time basis. I was so looking forward to having some form of normalcy in my life. I was determined to get back to my pre-cancer routine and feel whole again. Deepa was nervous about me going back to work and wanted me to wait. I was, however, determined that I could start seeing patients in the clinic and not do procedures. I started with my clinics. Many of my patients had been eagerly awaiting my return and were thrilled to see me. Things went smoothly for the first two weeks.

In early February, I felt sick again. It started with a sore throat. That sore throat soon turned into severe throat pain. I went to the emergency room in New Orleans to be checked out on February 5, 2019. Nothing was obviously wrong. Three days later, I developed a fever and cough and checked into a local hospital, where I was diagnosed with pneumonia affecting both my lungs. I stayed there for a few days with no improvement and was then transferred to MD Anderson in an ambulance. The day of my transfer was a miserable, rainy winter day. There had been many accidents on Interstate 10, resulting in a highway closure. The drive took over eight hours as we had to take side roads to bypass the closure. By the time I reached Houston on February 11th, I was extremely sick and needed acute care.

I underwent multiple tests at MD Anderson, including CT scans and a bronchoscopy. They found that I had a fungal infection of the larynx and the area around the vocal cords, causing severe pain. My pneumonia was thought to be viral in origin. They also suspected that I might be aspirating. I started a course of antibiotics, antiviral medications, and a high dose of antifungal treatments. The antifungals damaged my kidneys and made me extremely weak and sick. I was constantly nauseous and could hardly eat. Kidney failure was worrisome, and the kidney numbers fell into a troubling range. My weight plummeted again. I had no appetite and could not eat for weeks. This was when I dropped to the absolute lowest weight of my cancer journey—a mere 139 pounds (63 kilograms). I stayed in the hospital for nine days and was then discharged. I stayed in Houston for a few more days before returning home.

I realized that I needed more time to recover before returning to work.

On March 25th, the large catheter was finally removed. It was a big relief. It felt liberating. After three months, I could take a bath.

In April 2019, I returned to work for the second time. I started slowly and gradually increased my workload. By the summer of 2019, I was back performing procedures at the hospital. My doctors slowly tapered down my medications. I have remained well since then and have not needed to be hospitalized again for leukemia or its complications.

I did still make frequent visits to MD Anderson that year. There, I underwent many more bone marrow examinations, all of which showed normal results with no trace of leukemia. My donor's marrow has fully taken over my marrow. I had to undergo a series of immunizations. My new immune system was akin to a newborn's, and it had to be introduced to all the childhood and adult vaccines again.

Then, 2020 came with all its surprises. COVID-19 became a reality that affected everyone and took many lives. I needed to be incredibly careful during this time because I had an increased risk of COVID-19 complications due to my compromised immune system. I also desperately wanted to keep my newfound normalcy, so I took all possible precautions. At the beginning of the pandemic, I only did virtual care with audio and video calls. This soon became boring. That led me to return to the clinic despite the risk. We took all the contact and droplet precautions and thoroughly screened the patients at the reception for fever. I was not ready to give up my routine.

We lost many patients to COVID. Each loss felt terrible—I knew every one of them so well. They were like family to me. I called the families and shared their grief. I could not go to my patients' funerals, as I had in the past when time permitted. Our small community hospital was overwhelmed, and resources were stretched thin. My old hospital in Brooklyn was a COVID epicenter in New York City. Thousands in that community lost their lives. Many of my friends and colleagues got sick and had to be hospitalized. The chairman of medicine passed away, despite all heroic measures. Another cardiologist friend passed away.

In July 2020, I returned to MD Anderson for another checkup. I stayed at the Rotary House Hotel with Deepa and Soorya once again. On the day of my checkup, I woke up early and went out to the garden to mentally prepare myself for my days of tests.

My GVHD doctor was pleased with my progress. He said that he would see me once more in 2021. After that, I likely wouldn't need him anymore, though I would continue to have yearly visits with Dr. Caring. At this appointment, my bone marrow results were normal, with no traces of leukemia. My donor marrow was now producing all my blood cells. This was my twelfth bone marrow examination in two years and hopefully my last.

We soon returned home.

This drive would soon turn out to be different and consequential.

More surprises awaited me in the ensuing months and years.

Epiphany on Interstate 10

On that trip home in July 2020, Soorya drove. Deepa dozed off in the back. I sat in the front with Soorya. I had hours to think and reflect on my journey as the countryside passed by. I knew this swath of land and this road so well. This stretch of Interstate 10 held a special place in my life. I knew the bridges and even the metal artwork adorning the bridge railings. I knew the bayous it crisscrossed and the ultimate beauty of sunsets over the Atchafalaya Basin. I knew where to get the best coffee, hot dogs, or boudin. Boudin balls with jalapeno and pepper jack cheese were a treat from Don's Cajun eatery near Lafayette. I also knew where the clean toilets were. This highway had carried me through hell and back. If only one could tell the life stories these highways carry!

The interstate felt immensely bigger, broader, and more masculine in Texas. Once we crossed state lines, driving through the by-lanes and across paddy fields and sugarcane plantations, I breathed a sigh of relief. The condition of Louisiana's roads and the height of its buildings are not an accurate measurement of the heart of Louisiana. Undefinable, Louisiana is more spirit, an emotion emerging from its slower rhythm of life, which was palpable when I first arrived in 2008. The overwhelming feeling I have experienced here is unadulterated love. The kindness of these people is unending and has no boundaries. The culture is warm, welcoming, and the most soulful of anywhere I'd lived or traveled and unlike any place I have experienced, even having lived on three continents. Sadly, more people are leaving the state due to a lack of growth and opportunities, primarily for the bigger and bolder neighbor, Texas.

The state has hot, humid, steamy days and nights during the long, protracted summer. These miserable days and nights are merely a prelude to nature's dangerously destructive force, hurricanes. These earthly surrogates of fury are unleashed on the state ceremoniously year after year. Its cities and towns cautiously await this symbol of the ocean's wrath each summer. These storms originated off the shores of West Africa and carried water and air along the same path taken by thousands of bound and shackled slaves. When the winds made landfall, they unleashed their curses and anger with unimaginable destructive power. The howling winds are reminiscent of the cries of unbearable human pain.

❀

Somewhere along the drive home, as I gazed out at the countryside and thought about this home that fate had brought me to, I decided to write about my cancer experience. I had been keeping a small diary out of boredom while I was an inpatient and during my stays in Houston between hospital admissions. This diary would help me revisit and explore my emotions. I also knew that it would be emotionally taxing yet therapeutic, at the same time, and I was right.

More life experiences awaited me in 2020, 2021, and many more in 2023 and 2024. Some were pleasant and life-changing, while others were difficult and required help to get through them.

My body continued to heal, but my mind did not. The trauma of what I endured sometimes came back out of the dark corners of my mind and wrecked my spirit.

The Atomic Sands of Kerala and More Broken Clay Pots

Despite leaving the shores of Kerala, they had never left me, and my life abroad would be intertwined with life back in the village. The umbilical cord of affection and longing for the motherland was never severed. The temptation to return and serve my people became strong. This reality followed me all these years, including my years in America. The golden sand, the constant breeze from the ocean, and the ever-moving water kept calling me back. The monsoons came to my dreams and asked for my return. My mother's cooking and the aroma of finely ground spices were inviting. Much to Deepa's annoyance, my mom would let me eat out of the frying pan. The men and women who lived along the Arabian Sea and their life stories were a magnet, pulling me towards it. Year after year, I returned, like a pilgrimage. It kept me rooted in reality and helped me see what is essential in life. I'd missed years without wading into the sea of my childhood, my own amniotic fluid.

A voyage that took me from the lands of excess to a place of want and need. A place of stark and mind-numbing honesty. I looked forward to each trip and so did Deepa. As soon as the summer holidays started, she would be on a flight to Cochin International. These voyages continued during my British and American days.

My birthplace called to me like a caring siren. I needed to make up for lost time.

❖

My arrival was anticipated and well-publicized in the community. There would be no privacy. They had a long list of problems for me. Most involved monetary help from me. I was happy to oblige. Each time I returned, I heard and witnessed stories. These were not pretty stories; they were stories of struggles, disappointments, and tragedies.

And occasional triumphs. Like our childhood companion, Babu, who bought an auto rickshaw for himself. He was the youngest of six siblings. All of them grew up with us and worked among us. His parents also worked for us in the family compound, looking after paddy cultivation, and taking care of coconut plantations. He loved watching movies and never missed a new release at the local movie hall.

The local movie theater, Sri Muruga Theater, had different seating tiers. The cheapest was on the floor, on the sand, closest to the screen--that was where you would find Babu. The next tier was paved with concrete and had long wooden benches and individual chairs without padding or cushions. The final level, the luxury section, had reclining seats with cushions.

He would then recount the stories in full detail, without missing any specifics. He acted out the fights for us, completely animated. He went to school with us and soon found small jobs after high school. He then left for Chennai to work with his elder brother Krishnan, but the heat proved too much for him, and he eventually returned. He then got married, had children, and struggled for some time. He finally made enough money to buy an auto rickshaw, a considerable achievement. It cost him approximately 150,000 Indian rupees, which was nearly three thousand dollars at the time. Babu then became my mother's associate, running errands for her. Occasionally, he would take her to doctor's appointments and the nearest supermarket. Although these triumphs might seem trivial by American standards, they were considered a success story in this context.

Poverty affects one's statistical probabilities of living and dying, whether you die of natural or unnatural causes. For those of us who come from poor countries and live in poor states surrounded by impoverished people, we see a lot. Our destiny is to witness suffering unless we choose to walk away, eyes forever covered.

In some ways, it's akin to cancer. It's lived through, with no way to turn back the clock, doing what we can. I choose to help and heal others, which heals me in return. But I also learned that there is only so much you can do. It all felt like a drop in the ocean. The outcomes didn't change on a broader scale, though they did individually and for the small community. I have heard enough and seen enough on my trips home, and nothing shocked me anymore. There are many stories from the shore to pen down. It is beyond the scope of this book. It's hard not to be numbed by the gloomy news and hardships that abound.

I try to focus on the success stories: young people's successes in Kerala and abroad. I have friends who are business owners, and my family members have started companies on these shores and sent their children abroad to the finest universities in the United States and England. There are engineers, doctors, nurses, and airline employees. My family is also a shining example of success. My siblings have done very well in life. Their children did even better, most in the medical profession, being doctors or married to doctors. My twin brother established a company abroad, his children educated at premier universities in England.

These successes are only a fraction of what I saw and heard. There were many cancers in and around the village. On every trip I made back home, I saw cancer diagnoses and families struggling to care for cancer patients. In my immediate neighborhood alone, many of my friends and family members died of cancer. They were all in their forties or early fifties. Occasionally, I made these diagnoses, too, as in the case of Mr. Sajan, who ran a corner store next to a playground where we played volleyball. Mr. Sajan habitually checked his blood count and waited for my arrival. During one of my visits home, I saw that his counts were low and he needed a blood transfusion. I referred him to my classmate, an oncologist, who subsequently diagnosed him with myelofibrosis. He would soon develop leukemia and, unfortunately, pass away.

During my next visit, I had a memorable interaction with his mother. In her eighties, she eagerly awaited my arrival. She owned a thatched tea stall next to Mr. Sajan's shop for many years. She ran this stall with the help of her unmarried daughter, who had learning difficulties. They would be up early in the morning making tea and *puttu*, a local steamed rice cake. The fishermen who went to the sea before sunrise were their primary customers. To express her gratitude for helping her son, she invited me for tea at her shop.

The tea stalls in Kerala are unique. They use large metal teapots with a slow-burning fire underneath that burns continuously. Dried coconut shells are used for this burning. A coin is placed inside the pot, and the rattling of the coin then announces that the water is boiled. At her insistence, I sat on a wooden bench and watched her make the tea. She moved slowly and had severe scoliosis, her entire body curving to the right from the hip upwards. She wore a cotton blouse and a dirty white cotton lungi. Her silky white hair was now almost gone. Petite and frail, she was mostly skin and bones. Her sagging breasts hung outside the blouse, but she paid no notice to them. She had some leftover *puttu* and *kadala* curry from the morning serving, which she served me on an aluminum plate before serving the hot tea with milk.

The aluminum plate she served has seen better days. There were tiny little ants in the *puttu*. One by one, I picked them out discreetly so as not to upset my hostess. Soon, she bought the tea and sat next to me. Initially, she told me she was sad about losing her son and thanked me for helping him while wiping away her tears with the dirty lungi. Slowly, our conversation evolved, and she wanted to hear all about England and America. We continued talking as she rubbed my hand, looked intensely into my eyes, and listened to the stories. The large jumbo jets had fascinated her; she had never been on a train or a plane. The black and white people of America amused her. She had never seen a black person except on television. She told me she had seen white men and women when they passed her shop, either on a motorcycle or simply riding bicycles. The wooden stool we sat on was unsteady on the loose sand, and before I realized it, we both ended up on the ground, spilling the tea and the small plate of food she had served me. She fell backwards, hitting her spine on the floor first. I picked her frail body up, and she kept apologizing. Thankfully, she landed on sand, and there were no injuries.

On my next trip home, I returned to her with an automatic wrist blood pressure cuff made in the USA, which she highly appreciated.

Next door to Mr. Sajan lived another character we all loved who met an untimely death from cancer. Mr. Balan, Balettan as we called him, was spirited, joyful, and easygoing. He was a kid at heart who spread joy all around despite his difficult upbringing and hardship at work. He was one of the early emigrants to Saudi Arabia in the eighties. As a baker in Riyadh, he worked 12-hour shifts beside a furnace, making biscuits, bread, and pastries. It was hard work, and he always looked forward to the yearly vacation home. He told us stories of verbal and sometimes physical abuse of migrant workers in Saudi Arabia. "The local guys would spit on us." Women who worked as maids endured even worse abuse, including rape and physical violence.

He built a lovely concrete home on the land he inherited from his mother. His mother, in turn, was a single mother who worked in the local coir industry. Coir is made from coconut husks that are plentiful. When removed, these husks were kept underwater for a year in deep pits connected to the stream that passed along the house. These pits held water mostly neck deep and were large enough to hold thousands of these husks. The husks were then recovered and pummeled with wooden sticks to extract coir, which was dried under the sun and sold to exporters. Outside of fishing, many families worked in the coir industry. Women did most of the work. Most of the men were pit owners or supervisors. These women had to work neck-deep in the water beside men who employed them. The women had to dive to recover the husks, and were often subject to being touched without their consent, and worse.

Balettan was short yet well-built and pale-skinned, a complexion he inherited from his mother. He had a head full of black curly hair and a thick mustache. He wore Ray-Ban sunglasses with golden frames and smelled of perfumes. His petite wife, a tailor, stayed in the village, primarily working out of her house. She possessed a few skills outside of tailoring and had become a hit with local teenagers. This was common knowledge except for Balettan, who visited home yearly and stayed for a month or so. He had a Royal Enfield bike, which made a "put-put" noise, a status symbol that announced he had made it. He made use of the vacation like no one else. There were parties every night. Alcohol was not allowed in Saudi, so he overcompensated one month out of every year. One fine day, he returned early to Kerala for treatment and evaluation. He did not feel well and was losing weight. His wife called me, concerned, while I was in New York. A scan showed a mass in the liver. He had primary liver cancer and would soon pass away. He was in his late forties when he died.

Another young man also died of liver cancer in the immediate neighborhood. Ram lived two houses to the east of my house. A handsome, confident, and self-assured fellow, he lived with his parents and built a lovely two-story home. He wore the best perfumes and had thickly padded shoes to make him look taller; he was not short either. Many people knew him in Dubai, where he worked under the radar. He was well known to the Dubai police and immigration officials, as he sold bootleg alcohol to Indian and Pakistani workers.

The sale of alcohol is prohibited in most Middle Eastern countries. People were allowed to drink only in five-star hotels or resorts or needed a special permit, which cost money. So, the underground liquor business thrived. That is where Ram made money. He would often be caught selling alcohol and was jailed for brief periods. Authorities would soon expel him from the country. He would then make a fake passport, return to Dubai, and do it all over again. It was easy money. He sent money home to his elderly parents and never got married. He supported his extended family, took a few of his brothers and friends to Dubai, and settled them. He, too, came down with primary hepatocellular carcinoma; this time, the cause was clear: alcohol abuse and alcoholic cirrhosis. He was in his early forties when he died.

In 2010, my next-door neighbor, a 29-year-old, was diagnosed with primary lung cancer. He was a non-smoker and otherwise healthy. This development shocked us.

His brother Sanjeev was a close friend of mine, and together, we started a charitable establishment primarily to help cancer patients with local assistance. This will soon expand into other philanthropic activities, including financial assistance with education, wedding expenses, and the like. Surprisingly, the most frequently requested assistance was help with funeral arrangements. Many families have children living abroad who are making a living while leaving their elderly parents at home. As a result, providing immediate funeral assistance has greatly benefited the community. All the expenses were taken care of by the charitable society. After many years of effort, we were finally granted status as a Charitable Society, duly registered by the Government of India. This recognition will help us advance charitable activities, facilitate donations from abroad, build free old age homes, conduct medical camps, and more.

During the COVID pandemic, we maintained constant communication with the community and provided help, mostly in the form of financial aid for unemployed, poor, and grieving families. Local communities have rallied together, contributing a small sum to the fund every month. This initiative has ensured local representation, active participation, accountability, and sustainability. This model is now being replicated in other communities. It is a true blessing that, even on a smaller scale, we are in a position to improve the lives of our people.

Soon, the Government of India took notice. The government's atomic agencies conducted surveys based on the notion that cancer is highly prevalent in Kerala's coastal communities. They found that the Kerala coast has very high levels of radiation, possibly three times the average background radiation compared to the rest of India. There are elevated levels of thorium in the sand, which emits radiation. Uranium-containing granite is also prevalent in this region. This could explain the high incidence of cancer, including my own.

Those nights sleeping rough by the sea and years of living by the water may have come with a price. I had the added occupational radiation exposure while being an interventional cardiologist. This could explain why my twin brother was spared. We grew up next to each other, doing everything together as twins until we separated in our ways after college.

I will take you to my immediate neighborhood. The stories are troubling, and I feel inadequate and helpless whenever I think of these folks. Kerala also had a pattern that could be predicted. I call it "weddings and funerals." The two gentlemen you will read about next worked hard and did everything they could to support their families. Yet somewhere, they fell short and did the unthinkable.

Sundar, one of my father's cousins, ran a grocery store near our house, and lived two houses away from us. He had many siblings. His oldest brother did very well as a businessman in Sri Lanka. He was the first to fly in and out of the country in the 1960s. He visited us yearly. He flew from Colombo to Trichy in Tamil Nādu and then took a taxi across the state. It must have cost thousands of Indian rupees for that taxi ride. He and his wife had no children. One of Sundar's sisters lived in Mumbai. She and her children visited us during the summer holidays, and we became close by playing cricket. We heard all about the giant metropolis and life in the city from our cousins.

Another one of his brothers was a chef in Mumbai, with tons of stories. This brother had the habit of snuffing tobacco and smoking beedi. He returned poor from Mumbai. A few years ago, he developed nasopharyngeal cancer from tobacco usage and underwent radiation therapy. That was the last time I saw him and provided financial support. However, he would soon succumb to the disease.

Sundar was moderately successful in business. He was not astute, but he had a soft and kind spirit. Outside the grocery store, he ran a coir business and had additional income coming. He had two boys and three girls—a situation that often leads to challenges in some parts of India. The dowry system is still very prevalent. When girls get married, their parents are expected to provide a sack of money, a pot of gold, furniture, and utensils. When combined with the expense of a wedding, it can amount to thousands of dollars. Now, imagine multiplying this by three within five years. He had to borrow money. He was too proud and never asked us. Soon, the bank and the loan sharks were hounding him for repayment. After his third daughter was married, he was found slumped on the way to his home by his oldest son in the middle of the night. He drank a pesticide and could not be saved.

I was working in Scotland when I heard the news. It came while I was in the middle of my Membership (MRCP) exams, and Deepa couldn't bring herself to tell me about his death on the day it happened. She waited until my exams were over and I returned home. I was deeply upset. I knew him and his children very well. I was very fond of him. He was a simple, innocent man who was not skilled in business. He counted with his fingers and used an old-fashioned scale in his shop. He did too many favors and had difficulty saying no to people who came to his shop looking to buy essential items with no money. I was devastated that I hadn't been aware of his suffering and therefore hadn't been able to help.

His oldest daughter was married to a lovely person I had met many times. He worked for the Ritz-Carlton in Riyadh as a catering manager. He was clinically depressed, which was evident in his face from the moment I met him. Yet, he remained pleasant and humble. Shortly after his father-in-law committed suicide, he, too, took his own life. He and his wife, my cousin, had just celebrated their son's birthday. The oldest son took over his father's business but faced financial struggles after COVID-19 and even threatened suicide. We have been managing and navigating through his issues, and I am happy to say that he is in a much better place now.

My other neighbor, Vasu, was also a victim of the theme of weddings and funerals. Vasu had stayed with my grandfather in Trincomalee, Sri Lanka, while working on the plantations and was the only one present when my grandfather was dying from malaria. My grandmother and father were close to him because of this. He was a chef who had worked in a moderate-sized restaurant in Bengaluru, a cosmopolitan Indian city. We called him Vasuettan. This restaurant was purchased by one of my family members, Mr. Babu. He made his money in the alcohol business but recently passed away from alcoholic cirrhosis. He mostly hired village boys. The restaurant was in an upscale neighborhood called Malleswaram, near a roundabout. Vasu assisted the main chef. During my visit to the hotel, where I last saw him, he was in the kitchen slicing onions. At the time, he was a tall, skinny, fair-skinned man in his mid-50s. He had two daughters and no sons.

This father of two daughters was confident that he could easily arrange their marriages. However, he soon became sick, returned home, and struggled to pay for two weddings. He borrowed money from loan sharks who constantly harassed him. He hung himself from a long wooden beam in front of the house he had built for himself. His wife found him in the early hours of the morning.

Heart attacks happen at an alarming pace in Kerala and the rest of India. The mortality is alarmingly high, and increasingly, young men and women die from it, including my classmate, Sal. We went to school together and lived three houses to the east. His father was an army man who visited once a year. Sal was an entrepreneur who ran a successful tea stall on the street next to the Chennai railway station. He also had an alcohol outlet in Kerala, where his wife and children stayed. The business was thriving, and he had to recruit his brothers to join the company. He sold thousands of teas, vegetable cutlets, and samosas. His elder brother had already passed away after sustaining a heart attack a few years ago. The last time I saw Sal, he had gained a lot of weight—a sign of him doing well in my part of the country.

One evening, he started having chest pain. He knew that this could be a heart attack, having witnessed his brother's experience. Instead of seeking immediate medical attention, he took the next train to Kerala to be with his wife and children. It was an overnight journey. He followed his brother's example, who had done the same. By the time he reached Kerala, his condition had worsened, and he soon died of cardiac arrest.

There are many more stories from the shore to pen down. It is beyond the scope of this book. As you can see, these stories are intertwined with my life story. I took them personally and grieved for these folks. Their sorrows became mine. Part of me never left these beautiful shores where death and sickness danced to the tunes of the Arabian Sea. The land smelled of tragedy and despair, despite its indescribable beauty and solitude. The younger generation has largely moved away to break the shackles of poverty and misery. Soon, it will become an empty landscape, inhabited only by a few fishermen and those who could not travel or move abroad. Many bird species and animals that we never saw growing up have returned and now inhabit the deserted land. A family of peacocks lived on our land and slept on the terrace next to my bedroom. I watched them secretly through the window and the curtains. My mother and the caretaker fed them and enjoyed their company, despite the noise that accompanied it. I saw an armadillo, a fox, and a few wild boars beside my family compound. Added to that is a family of long-necked swans and many different species of birds with which I am unfamiliar. They are reclaiming the land. Sightings of leopards are all too common now on the mainland of Kerala. The value of coconut has plummeted; hence, the plantations, once a lifeline for the entire state of Kerala, are now abandoned.

Yes, I was living in world capitals and socializing with elites, yet a part of me carried the sorrow of my homeland. There was a lot of sorrow, and time only made it worse. The monsoon rains washed the land of pain and suffering, and the streams carried it out to the sea. They remained silent, preserving their innocence, waiting for the monsoons, and watching generations come and go—holding a front-row seat to the cycle of life and death on the shores.

I share these stories and litanize the names of my friends and neighbors to bear witness, to honor their lives and personhood. I was one of the lucky ones. I still am. There's no way to repeat this enough.

The Big Reveal

Humans have evolved over many millennia, though we only know the history of the last few thousand years. Many individuals have stood out in history due to their attributes and ingenuity. There were conquerors and war heroes, artists, painters, and musicians. There were poets and novelists, as well as sages and gods. Some men and women wove the world together with a common thread--an emotion or attribute that is difficult to define. This quality has existed since the beginning of time and has immortalized a few chosen men and women. Some went on to become gods and sages because of this quality. Jesus Christ serves as a prime example of this virtue. In the end, this emotion is what has held the world together. Like a river with no beginning and end, it has flowed through our minds and hearts for countless generations. It is the true spirit of kindness. Throughout history, we have seen examples of men and women, kings and gods, performing acts of kindness. It is the greatest gift to mankind. It originates within you and me. It is never-ending, and it defines you and your essence.

On July 16, 2020, Deepa and I spoke with our stem cell transplant coordinator at MD Anderson. We thought it was time to contact my donor and thank him. We had waited two years since we were still unsure about the outcome of my transplantation. We didn't want to expose the donor to what could be a bad outcome. We were also not ready to deal with the emotional roller-coaster ride that came along with the prospect of meeting the donor. Possible rejection would indeed be hurtful, and we have heard of situations where donors wanted to remain anonymous. However, we would think nothing less of our donor.

The past few months were difficult for us emotionally, as Soorya has changed his life plans. Earlier that year, he decided to take a break from his medical studies and pursue a career with the United States Air Force. Deepa and I were excited for him, but we were not looking forward to him shipping out for training and being away from us for years. He was determined to pursue it. It seemed like a natural progression for him. He wanted to pursue this ambition despite knowing the challenges of military life. Deepa stood by him and took him to the recruitment center. While she was scared for him, she was also happy that Soorya was following his dreams. He would be part of the world's greatest military, serving alongside brave men and women with honor and dignity. We are humbled and proud that our only son will serve this great nation and uphold its ideals.

Contacting a donor is a two-way process mediated by the NMDP. Both sides must agree to be contacted. It is an emotional process, and one needs to be ready to face the feelings it brings to the surface. At our request, the transplant coordinator sent us the paperwork that would give the donor permission to contact me. I signed the paperwork and returned it to the coordinator the same day.

I was at work on Friday, July 31, 2020, when the transplant coordinator called me from Houston around 8:30 in the morning. She sounded ecstatic. She said that the donor had agreed to be contacted and that she would forward the donor's details to me. His name was Andrew Chuisano, and he lived in New Jersey. The name caught me off guard. I was not expecting a Caucasian name. I was expecting an Indian or Asian name instead. I already knew he was twenty-four years old when he donated the marrow that saved my life.

I resolved to call him as soon as I could process my emotions.

Despite knowing nothing about him, I could tell he cared deeply about others and understood human suffering. He knew of the vulnerability of being human. With his life-saving donation, he carried forward the human tradition of kindness.

Monday, August 17, 2020, started as a typical workday for me. I had finally worked up the courage to communicate with Andrew. It has been two weeks since I had his contact information. That morning, in between seeing patients, I sent him an email.

Andrew,
This is Deepak Thekkoott.
I am the recipient of your marrow from June 2018.
I am letting you know that I am alive after 2 years, and your marrow is working. I had a very difficult 2 years with Acute Myeloid Leukemia, and the transplantation course was also hard on my body.

I am an Interventional Cardiologist in Louisiana, from Baton Rouge. I am originally from South India. My wife is Deepa, and our son, Soorya, 26, has joined the Air Force and will start his training next month.

Andrew, we are and will forever be grateful to you.

We are also thankful to your family and friends. My family, friends, and coworkers also extend their deep appreciation for your selfless act.
Your selflessness has reinforced our faith in humanity.

If that's okay, we would like to schedule a video call at a convenient time for both of us.

Deepak
Cell xxxxxxxxx

I wondered whether he would write back.

Andrew responded by noon.

Mr. Thekkoott,
I am beyond thankful to hear the news that you are doing well! My twin sister (Megan) battled leukemia, had a stroke, and recently had a heart transplant, so I've seen how hard the battle can be.

Your son is my age, that's very exciting, he will be taking a great career path!

Video chatting is fine with me, I am located in NJ. Would you like tonight if that works with your schedule?

Thanks- Andrew

*Please excuse typos, sent from a mobile device

Andrew himself was also a twin. His twin sister, Megan, had leukemia when she was a teenager and needed a bone marrow transplant. Andrew was tested to be a potential donor; however, he was not a match for his sister, but his elder brother was. She thankfully made it through all the difficulties of her treatment, which I was happy to hear. Andrew then offered to video chat or FaceTime with me that evening.

When I got home that evening, I broke the news to Deepa. Soorya was home as well, and he also wanted to join the call. At seven o'clock, Andrew called. We opened FaceTime promptly.

We experienced an immediate and profound connection. It isn't easy to describe the rush of emotions I felt. Andrew was all smiles; he had the biggest grin. He, too, was excited to see me. Andrew was now twenty-six but looked much younger, more like a teenager or a college student. He told us that he was a police officer in a small town in New Jersey and had been with the police force for the last six years. He told us he was also the first match the transplant service had contacted.

The call from the donor matching program had come in after

hours. Being a cop, he got a fair number of unwanted calls. He had a habit of declining calls from unfamiliar numbers. However, he hesitated when this particular call came in from an unknown number. "They kept calling," he said. "Something told me to answer this call." It was the NMDP. Andrew was in their registry because he had been tested years earlier when his sister had cancer.

Andrew and his twin sister hadn't been a match, yet he and I were. It was a full and perfect match.

He did not hesitate and agreed to be my donor on the spot. Just like that, in an evening conversation between two unknown people, Andrew helped save the life of another total stranger going through a life-or-death crisis in another part of the country.

Andrew's mannerisms were sweet, wonderful, and polite. I could tell that he was happy in his life. It radiated from his face, his posture, and his gestures. Agreeing to be a donor came naturally to him. He didn't think much of it and was not looking for any adulation. He knew my difficult journey, having watched his own sister on hers.

During our call, he also spoke to Deepa and Soorya. He was happy for Soorya, who was soon leaving to join the Air Force. We also met Andrew's girlfriend, Jenna. They lived together, along with Andrew's cat, Trigger.

We had yet to envision the life-altering impact of this call. Just like that, one summer evening in 2020, we connected. I was connecting with my life source. A source who had performed a life-sustaining intervention for me, not knowing anything about me: it was a miracle. I was emotional, and so was Deepa. Andrew was casual and talked to us like he knew us from before, as if we were no strangers.

"Deepak," Andrew said, "I would do it all over again. This is the easiest way one could save a life," Andrew said casually, and he meant it. It was all in a day's work for him. "Wouldn't you?"

"Yes, I would do it a thousand times over," I said, "after what you did for me."

We ended the call by promising to keep this relationship going and thanking him and his family again.

Andrew and Soorya became acquainted and discussed the Air Force boot camp and police academy. We were happy that we made the decision to connect. In the months and years to come, our bond deepened. Andrew visited us in Louisiana in 2021. Autumn of 2022 saw us traveling to Morristown, New Jersey for Andrew and Jenna's wedding. It was a beautiful ceremony. Andrew's favorite aunt officiated the wedding, and we danced to the music. We met family and friends from both sides. We met Megan, Andrew's twin sister, and fell in love with her.

Kindness holds the world together. The glue that makes us stick together and look out for each other. It flows through our hearts with no beginning or end. It is the greatest of virtues. The expression of the Universe within us.

The Eurasian Connection

My call with Andrew got me thinking about those who came before me, about distant ancestors who made the trek out of Africa, the cradle of human life. It is possible that some of those ancestors are also related to Andrew.

The circumstances leading to this unusual union between Andrew and me—his bone marrow now residing within me—are hard to fathom. I don't think I will ever be able to completely understand or explain how it is that we should originate in different corners of the world and yet find commonality in our genetic structure. It's just too mathematically improbable. And yet, our HLA markers were a perfect match—ten out of ten.

HLA markers are intricately linked to one's genealogy and ancestry. Andrew is of Mediterranean/Italian heritage. His grandfather emigrated to the United States from Sicily. Hence, he is a second-generation Italian American. On the other hand, I am of South Asian/Indian heritage. It is exceedingly rare—nearly impossible, in fact—to find a match outside one's ethnic origin.

Then, the fact that we were twins. Our life situations were so very dissimilar yet also similar in many ways. Andrew, growing up, had to deal with his twin sister battling leukemia. I went through hell and back, fighting the same curse.

I wonder if I will ever find the truth or the science behind these rarest occurrences. And yet, I started looking for answers anyway. The possibility of a common ancestry between Andrew and me intrigued me. While it was possible for me to match with a Caucasian simply due to the astronomical number of HLA pools available in the registry for those of Caucasian ancestry, it was unbelievably unlikely. This defied the logic of mathematics. It seemed more like pure chance. So, I started looking for answers beyond this extremely rare mathematical possibility and the vagaries of fate. This led me to trace my own and Andrew's ancestries through the ages.

The exact age of the human race is still unclear. We undoubtedly date back hundreds of thousands of years. It is thought that humans evolved as a species on the eastern African seaboard. The first human migration out of Africa started between 100,000 and 150,000 years ago. What prompted humans to migrate is still unclear, though the most likely explanations are a change in the climate, a lack of food, and over-population.

The first migration was slow. It moved from the Horn of Africa into the Arabian Peninsula. From there, the migration continued into southern Asia, southeastern Asia, and Australia. Many Indians, especially those from South India, are descended from this first migration out of Africa. These first inhabitants of India are known as the Dravidians.

A second migration saw humans travel north from Africa into Eurasia. From there, this population, known today as Caucasians—named for the mountainous Caucasus Region that spans the Middle East and Eastern Europe—diverged between 20,000 and 40,000 years ago. One group turned west and north into the Mediterranean region and then continued into the Nordic countries and the current British Isles. The other group turned east and migrated to India through what is now Iran, Afghanistan, and Pakistan. This group mainly settled in northern India and contributed to what is called the Indian Aryan civilization.

This divergence is why Caucasian genes are widespread today across northern India, Afghanistan, Pakistan, Iran, and Europe. These genes are also often found among southern Indians like me due to population mixture and migration within India.

Almost at the same time, there was another wave of migration through the Asian plains. It passed through Mongolia and China and into present-day Russia. Many of these people then crossed the land bridge that stretched across the Bering Strait and continued down through Canada. This wave of migration would go on to populate both North and South America. This was the longest migration in human history, carrying humans from Africa to South America by land. It began approximately 100,000 years ago; the southernmost tip of South America was settled by these migrants approximately 13,000 to 20,000 years ago.

Human migration and the genetic mixture that comes from it have continued throughout recorded history, especially with some of the large wars the world has witnessed. These prolonged conflicts have resulted in population movements since at least 500 BCE. These wars have involved many kingdoms and dynasties. The expansion of the Persian Empire and the movement of its people was the first major population movement across Eurasia and the Mediterranean in recorded history. The campaigns of Alexander the Great followed this. The expansion of these kingdoms contributed to the spread of different genes to the Indian subcontinent. Because of these various population movements, historical conquests, and the resultant mixing of peoples, India has one of the most diverse gene pools on Earth.

In the last few hundred years, this movement of people has only increased and picked up speed. The European invasion of the Americas and their bringing vast numbers of Africans to North and South America as slaves are just two such examples of this.

In modern-day genetics, the study of and ideas about genealogy are still evolving. We now know that gene pools around the world are constantly evolving due to the mixture of cultures and civilizations. The analysis of human DNA by various organizations like the Human Genome Project has now established a vast database of gene pools, from which one can identify their exact ancestry, even down to minute details. Thanks to these scientific projects, there are now many commercially available ancestry services, such as 23andMe and Ancestry.com's AncestryDNA, which can help one learn more about one's genetic origins.

My quest to understand and explore the genetic possibilities of my HLA being compatible with Andrew's took me nowhere. I asked my transplantation doctor and other specialists if they had any insights. They all told me that we must share a common ancestor at some point far, far back in our genetic family trees. This was the most likely explanation. Otherwise, it would simply be an extremely rare occurrence of random chance.

Then came the next surprise.

As I continued my research, I realized that I had over three thousand potential matches in the bone marrow donation registry. That didn't seem right. That number seemed astronomically large. I suspected that the actual number was three hundred and that an extra zero had been added by mistake. I emailed my transplant coordinator, asking for clarification on the number. She emailed me back, saying that this number was accurate. I had close to three thousand potential matches in the donor registry. Usually, she said, a transplant coordinator gets as many as ten matches to work with, even for Caucasians looking for a match. Having this many matches is extraordinarily uncommon and difficult to explain.

All I can conclude is that I have possibly one of the most common HLA patterns in the world, despite being of South Indian origin. Finding a genetic commonality with Andrew was a rarity in itself; matching with three thousand or so potential donors was inexplicable to me and will remain a mystery.

Facing such a vast surprise, my quest for answers came to a halt. There was more at play here than Andrew and I having a common ancestor.

Our ancestors already set much of what happened between Andrew and me in motion. We had no roles to play, as our genetic structure is the culmination of many thousands of years of living by hundreds of generations of ancestors. We are branches of the tree of life.

This unlikely union causes me to thank my ancestors. I wish I knew all of them so I could personally thank them. I wish I knew their life circumstances and who our common ancestor was.

Looking at my family, I suspect that my paternal grandmother and her lineage may have been the source of our genetic commonality. This is just my theory, and I cannot prove it, but I do know that I inherited her genes by virtue of my features and my light skin tone. My grandmother was extremely fair-skinned, with a complexion similar to a Caucasian woman who had applied a bronze tan over her body, much like a Mediterranean-tanned skin tone. She passed that on to my father and, ultimately, to me. In fact, I had the palest and the lightest skin in my school. Our mannerisms were also remarkably similar. We both saw the world through a lens of kindness. We both wanted to do good for humanity.

My grandmother died in July 2004 at ninety-six. We have no record of her ancestry. Even so, I am certain that she is smiling down on me from the heavens and perhaps had a hand in putting my miraculous recovery through my miraculously matchable genes.

I have accepted that I may never fully know or comprehend what happened and what forces were at play in my ancestry and genetics. I am just grateful to my ancestors for this lucky combination of events across the generations that gave me a second chance at life.

This random miracle of things is what the Universe does when you least expect it. The Universe reminds you from time to time that she oversees your experience on Earth and that our collective lack of understanding of the Universe is as colossal and vast as the Universe itself.

My search for answers on genetic commonality made me think about my genetic structure. My genetic credentials are different from what I came to life with. Modern science has saved my life by artificially changing it, making me an aberration of the Universe—a human Chimera!

The Chimera in Me

A monster with a lion's head, a goat's body, and a serpent's tail, a chimera breathes fire. The term represents or describes an individual or organism produced by mixing and combining varied species or beings.

Homer described the Chimera in his ancient epic, the Iliad, saying that she was of divine origin, not a mortal, with the front part resembling a lion, the rear resembling a serpent, and the middle part a goat, fiercely breathing out the power of blazing fire. This intriguing mythological description leads me to consider the medical idea of human chimeras.

These are individuals who carry two separate sets of genetic markers. The most common human chimeras are those who have received stem cell transplants. I have two sets of DNA, and that makes me a human chimera. In my case, I still carry my own DNA in my tissues, including my hair, teeth, skin, bones, and other tissues. I also carry Andrew's DNA in my blood. All my blood cells are produced with and have his DNA. Andrew's DNA might also appear in other parts of my body as time passes. So, clearly, I am walking around with two sets of DNA inside me. Modern medicine has transformed me into a different person than I was originally.

Challenges come with the fact that many humans are walking around with two distinct DNAs. They seem to happen more often in crime scene analysis. DNA analysis has wrongfully accused bone marrow transplant recipients of crimes their bone marrow donors commit-ted and vice versa. This has become a problem in DNA analysis as more and more patients receive stem cell transplants. If I were to commit a crime and leave blood behind at the crime scene, DNA analysis would show that the incriminating blood belonged to Andrew. This has hap-pened in some astonishing cases. In one case of sexual assault, DNA analysis indicated that the crime was committed by a felon who was already behind bars at the time of the crime. Investigators soon realized that his brother was the real culprit; the brother who committed the crime had donated bone marrow to the felon before his conviction and imprisonment.

Currently, commercially available chromosome and ancestry ser-vices like Ancestry.com and 23AndMe also have difficulty differentiat-ing between the two sets of DNA found in a person who has undergone stem cell transplantation. Inaccurate and/or incomplete results are com-mon in these circumstances.

Things have become even more complex with patients who have received umbilical cord blood transplants. In such cases, the donor's identity is kept secret. When patients who have received cord blood transplants participate in chromosomal or genetic testing, they will be identified as immediate family members of folks from remote lands who have no family connections whatsoever. This could lead to interesting situations.

Sometimes, in even stranger cases, children are born with none of their mother's DNA. These children carry their father's DNA and that of a completely different, though related, person. These true hu-man chimeras occur when the mother is born with two different sets of DNA. This rarity happens when the mother in question acquires the DNA of her unborn miscarried twin in the womb. This unborn twin exists only in the mother's DNA, often hiding in the ovaries and mater-nal eggs. This DNA will then be transferred to the child, along with the father's DNA, thus causing the actual mother to be genetically unrelat-ed to the child. Understandably, this can cause significant problems in family dynamics and has led to protracted court cases.

Out of curiosity, I had my DNA analyzed three separate times by different companies. Unfortunately, all three tests yielded no results due to these platforms' inability to process my two sets of DNA.

More exciting developments are happening along the lines of chimera. These human-animal, mostly human-pig, chimeras are artificially created by adding human stem cells into animal embryos. These animals then grow and have organs that can be harvested and used for human transplantation with a reduced chance of rejection. History was made in January 2022 when a Maryland man received a genetically modified pig heart and lived for two months, creating a window for future animal organ transplantation. Since then, there have been more cases like that.

Chimeras are an aberration in the Universe. Unlike the mythical creatures that needed to be killed by the all-time best slayer of monsters in ancient Greece, Bellerophontes, modern-day chimeras are spitting hope instead of fire. Those of us who became chimeras by a stem cell transplant are just as cool as the descriptions in the Iliad. We are here to stay.

Dreams and More Dreams

My nights changed. They were not the same as they had been before my cancer.

At some point in 2020, I noticed something happening to me when I slept. I started having vivid dreams. All kinds of dreams. But they all had one thing in common: they never ended well. I would wake up multiple times a night, sweaty and panicky. Invariably, my heart would be racing. I would then return to a very superficial sleep and soon repeat the process. My dreams terrified me. These were the kind of dreams that no one wanted. They took me back to my worst memories. The traumas I had experienced throughout my life were reenacted so vividly. I saw the family members I had lost over the years. I saw my father. In one dream, I was giving him CPR all by myself. That dream ended with him dying in my arms. I relived the complications I had experienced in the procedures I had performed over the years and the ensuing trauma. I saw the patients who died under my hands. I was bitten by venomous snakes and rabid dogs, trampled by elephants, and hit by trains. I fell off cliffs and drowned in deep oceans. Then there were the ones that filled me with deep shame, like walking the streets in daylight with minimal or no clothing. My heart raced and pounded through these dreams. They didn't come every night, but they happened more nights than not. My sleep was affected, and it made me tired during the day.

I dreaded going to bed each night. I didn't know how to deal with this new development.

I told Deepa about my dreams, and she recommended discussing them with Dr. Caring on our next visit, and we did. I started explaining what was happening to me. Before I finished my sentence, Dr. Caring touched my arm. "You are experiencing post-traumatic stress disorder." She recommended I seek counseling. A cancer diagnosis, with its prolonged treatments and the uncertainty of the outcome, is traumatic to the mind and soul. The reality of one's tenuous mortality, coupled with the trauma imparted on the body by surgery, radiation, and chemotherapy, will surely affect the mind and can manifest as PTSD later.

The medical world is finally making the connection between surviving cancer and PTSD, which can manifest in a myriad of ways: anxiety, depression, and a barrage of emotions based on the extent of the trauma. According to recent studies, up to one-third of cancer patients can manifest symptoms of PTSD during or after treatment. Depression is even more common; half of all patients may develop depression resulting from the diagnosis and treatment of cancer.

AML is an especially difficult cancer. It can impart trauma in many ways due to the complexity of the disease, poor prognosis, and prolonged treatment, including the overly complex and often challenging journey through stem cell transplantation. There is still not enough done to deal with this possible lingering side effect of intense treatment.

Researchers now recommend concurrent psychotherapy or emotional support while undergoing treatment—especially bone marrow transplantation—to reduce the aftereffects of depression and PTSD. In my case, I was not even forewarned about the possibility of developing PTSD.

Dr. Caring recommended Dr. Mike Klaybor. Based in Houston, Dr. Klaybor treated many physicians and surgeons with PTSD, and doctors from MD Anderson, other than Dr. Caring, vouched for his expertise. Cancer doctors deal with mortality and suffering more than any other medical specialty. They deal with life and death daily. Ideally, all physicians should understand this vulnerability. We are no different from other humans. Instead, we are more vulnerable simply because we care for others. We have a caring heart. That is why we became physicians in the first place. Being a physician comes with an enormous price.

Currently, some medical licensing bodies have it wrong. There are medical societies out there with archaic and unfriendly statutes that discourage physicians from seeking mental health care. Instead of this backward-looking practice, they should mandate regular mental health check-ins for stress, anxiety, depression, and PTSD. This is essential self-care, especially in light of the epidemic of physician suicides in the United States—a reality I know from personal experience.

Over the years, I have seen very accomplished residents, physicians, and even senior-level medical staff, like professors, succumb to depression, substance or alcohol abuse, and even suicide. A dear friend had to undergo rehab for alcohol use before he could continue practicing. I also knew a surgical resident who staged his suicide to look like a murder. Imagine the depth of despair one must feel to fake a suicide just to save face for the family left behind. That is the only reason I can think of. I knew his father, who was also a doctor. It is said that on average, one physician commits suicide in this country every day. Suicidal ideations are rampant among physicians, and there is an epidemic of depression among medical students.

Procedure complications and death from procedures have evoked unexplainable feelings of guilt and shame in me. I took them very personally and would be sad for days after serious complications, even though I tried to hide it. There are no tests or procedures in medicine that are absolutely risk-free. Mistakes and adverse reactions can always happen, especially if you are overworked or not at your best. I have had my fair share of mishaps.

One such mistake will never leave me. I was on call for general medicine on a cold January night in the Welsh country. It was a district hospital with a bustling emergency room. I was working in cardiology, though we shared calls with general medicine. The call started on Friday evening and ended on Sunday evening with six hours of rest or sleep time. Forty-eight-hour calls were common in those days. That particular weekend, no one could cover the shift from Sunday night until Monday morning. Reluctantly, I agreed to take that shift. I had a senior house officer and a house officer to assist me, with consultants available at home for advice or help.

On Friday, a tall, muscular, handsome young fellow came to the ER with a fever. He underwent routine bloodwork and other necessary evaluations and was stable. The house officer assured me there was nothing suspicious. The senior house officer on call also reviewed the patient. By then, at least two physicians and a house officer saw him, including an emergency room physician. He was soon discharged from the emergency room with a prescription for Tylenol. This young patient was well-received in the ER because he was a rugby player for the Welsh team. A celebrity in the Rugby world.

That night, the cardiac arrest pager went up sometime in the middle of the night, and I rushed to the ER. It was the same rugby player who was brought in for a cardiac arrest by ambulance. He was pulseless and clammy. We worked hard on him, but couldn't save his life. He had pink and red blotchy rashes on his body. I noticed that during CPR.

His death caused a furor in Wales as he was a well-known player. The news of his untimely death came in the local press and on TV, including the BBC. The death was interpreted as a misdiagnosis. The family was upset and asked for further inquiries. An autopsy later confirmed meningococcal meningitis. His fever was from meningitis, though he had no signs or symptoms suspicious of meningitis except fever. This is typical of meningococcal meningitis, a near-fatal disease if not diagnosed early enough. These patients can decline rapidly into septic shock and eventually into cardiac arrest, as happened here. No one could have predicted that.

That same weekend, I was called into the emergency room to evaluate a patient with pneumothorax. It was Sunday night by then, nearing the end of my marathon call. I had been on call since Friday night and had to deal with the cardiac arrest of the rugby player. This patient with pneumothorax was nearing "tension status," the nurses told me.

Pneumothorax happens when there is a spontaneous puncture in the lung's lining, causing air to leak out of the lungs into the chest cavity. It could also be due to trauma. The punctured lung and the air leaking out into the chest cavity cause displacement and compression of the heart and lungs. For this reason, a ventilator is not advised, as it would cause more air to leak into the chest cavity as the machine pushes oxygen into the lungs. The immediate, life-saving treatment involves placing a chest tube into the chest cavity to relieve pressure on the lungs. The tube is typically left in place for several days until the leak has stopped and the lungs have healed. This is an emergency procedure, and if not performed promptly, it could result in the patient losing their life.

The hospital catered for Rhondda Valley in Wales, which had a large population of coal miners. Respiratory illness was an active issue among miners, who often had bad lungs. This patient was a miner who couldn't breathe and had a history of respiratory problems resulting from his job. I was told that he was very sick, and the nurses had prepped him for a chest tube. I rushed into the procedure room in the emergency department to attend to the patient, who was struggling to breathe and in severe distress. An X-ray was displayed on a viewer on the wall opposite the patient. The pneumothorax appeared to be on the patient's left side. Little did I know or suspect that this X-ray positioning created an illusion. Nurses prepped the left side of the patient's chest. A junior nurse was scrubbed and standing ready for me by the bedside. The nurse in charge of the emergency department stood by her and helped her set up the procedure.

The patient was struggling to breathe and was in a clammy state. I felt an impending doom. I can vividly visualize that senior nurse, even to date, standing by the wall, next to the patient's feet, and advising the junior nurse. They were tired, too. It was well past midnight, and I was barely functioning, having been on call since Friday night. My job is to make a nick in the chest wall and introduce a chest tube to relieve the pressure from the lungs. He was nearing what we call tension pneumothorax and could go into respiratory shock at any time.

I soon went to the left side of the patient and marked my puncture site. The nurse passed me the lidocaine to numb the chest wall. I explained to the patient what I was doing to him and promised him that once the tube was in, he would feel a lot better. I then injected the lidocaine into the marked site on the left chest wall without any difficulties. Then I asked for the scalpel.

Before I made the incision with the scalpel, I took another look at the X-ray. Something prompted me to do the same. I was watching the patient's breathing pattern and saw that his left chest wall was moving, not the right. That made me suspicious, and I took another look at the X-ray.

I gasped and stopped. I looked at the charge nurse in disbelief. "Oh my God," I whispered to her, not to worry the patient. "We are working on the wrong side of the patient."

I still get the same horror I felt that night in Wales whenever I think about this case. I was standing on the wrong side to do the procedure on this sick patient in his extremes. The X-ray was placed on the wall towards the patient's foot, and that deceived the nurses into selecting the proper side. The pneumothorax was on the right side. Placing the X-ray towards the patient's foot gave the illusion that pneumothorax was on the left side. I trusted the nursing staff, though I would have been more cautious and prudent on a day when I was fresher and less tired. My judgment fell short, too. I immediately apologized to the patient, switched the side, and then put the chest tube on the patient's right side where the pneumothorax was situated. He felt better in no time. There were more surprises for him. The repeat X-ray came as a surprise. He now has a new pneumothorax on the left side. It was most likely induced by me while injecting lidocaine, not to mention that his lungs were pushed to the left side by the tension on the right side of the chest cavity. I placed another chest tube on the left side.

He left the emergency room with two chest tubes instead of one, clearly not an ideal situation. The difficult job was explaining all this to his son in the wee hours of the morning, including my near-fatal mistake. I distinctly remember the son's response, who, in turn, asked me in his polite Welsh way. "Thank you for taking care of our father. Is he going to be okay ?"

All I could do was apologize to him and the patient. Luckily, he did well and was discharged home, unlike the rugby player who came in that weekend.

Medical mishaps can and will happen, especially in a system that pushes doctors to the brink. Sheer exhaustion, lack of support, low morale, and unrealistic expectations will lead to physician burnout. Doctors are in a tough, non-forgiving environment. In many advanced and poor countries, the appetite for studying medicine is falling due to the above reasons, even though the world needs more physicians as we age.

Healing with Help

I reached out to Dr. Mike Klaybor on the same day of the visit with Dr. Caring. Sitting in one of the gardens, I called him from outside the hospital entrance. I explained my situation and what I was feeling. Despite his extremely busy schedule, he graciously accepted me as a patient. We arranged video consultations, which were convenient during the COVID-19 pandemic and helped me avoid travel. The relationship formed then, and sessions over the ensuing years blossomed into a strong bond between me and Dr Klabor. I addressed him as "Mike," both politely and affectionately. It has been a blessing.

We started with two or three sessions a week and gradually, over several months, tapered down to one session a week. Currently, I'm down to one session every six to eight weeks.

There are many interventions and treatments for PTSD. Medications play a limited role. Cognitive behavioral therapy (CBT) is one type of treatment for PTSD, and that is what Mike recommended and used with me. Together, Mike and I revisited my trauma multiple times and in great depth. He asked me to take the time to grieve for myself. I realized that I had not yet grieved what had happened to me. I had consciously suppressed my grief, and as a result, I had feelings of guilt, shame, and sadness. I avoided stressful situations, lacked pleasure in life, felt distant from people, and lost interest in almost all the things I enjoyed before my cancer diagnosis. I had difficulty falling and staying asleep. I often re-lived some of my most difficult days and would suddenly experience a state of terror. Discussing my diagnosis and revealing my current cancer status caused great sadness. I choked up often while discussing my leukemia experience with my family, friends, and patients. I was suppressing my feelings instead of facing them. I went back to work too soon after my treatment and hoped these feelings would disappear. Now, with Mike's help, I understood that this had been a mistake.

Together, we dug deep into my negative emotions, exploring and dissecting them. We recorded the details of my present emotional state, which was filled with sadness and had little room for happiness. Pleasure seemed to elude me. I was in denial about what had happened to me, and a sense of shame engulfed me. In a way, I felt guilty about my cancer. I consciously hid my diagnosis from my close friends, revealing it only to a few in the US. The past two years of cancer and recovery have changed me profoundly.

Once we had documented my current emotional state, Mike asked me to modify these negative emotions and sentiments by rewriting my cancer story and ending on a positive note. We read these revised notes aloud. He made an audio file of my newfound positivity through words and phrases. He asked me to listen to this recording as often as I could. We listened to it together.

These are some of my reframed thoughts:

My family loves me and will stand by me.
Confident and loved.
I have made my family feel secure.
Proud.
I have achieved a lot in my life. I have shown my son how to live and made my wife feel secure.
Relieved.
I was better positioned to deal with my cancer than anyone in my family would be.

Positive and optimistic.
Compassion and empathy will help me heal.
Positive.
I can find people who will positively influence my healing.
Optimistic
My mother was happy to hear I was doing well.
Relieved.

From these notes documenting my reframed thoughts, I put together a mantra I recited as often as possible. It helped pull my mind from the depths of sorrow and sadness. I had to break the chains of my bondage, which were formed from negativity and angst. The trauma was deep, and I resisted initially, but this mantra ultimately helped.

I am beating this cancer with my new, calming, rational beliefs.
This is a bad dream that will pass.
This is a passing phase in my life, and I will come through it.
My cancer diagnosis has brought me calm.
I'm aware of my mortality and take each day as it comes.
My mind is more prepared for anything that may happen in my life.

Discussing, digging deep into, and exploring one's hidden emotions can be painful. Analyzing a single emotion can take a whole therapy session. But eventually, doing so will lead to a better place. We must do our best to be honest with ourselves and our feelings and understand their origins as a path to reorient thoughts, bending them toward the positive.

Just as doctors can help heal bodies, therapists can guide us to healing our minds. This whole process requires the help of an experienced therapist. One must also be ready to accept the emotions it will bring to the surface. I felt vulnerable.

I had never been in therapy before, but my sessions with Mike opened my eyes to a new therapeutic arena, which is immensely powerful and soulful.

In my sessions, we also discussed my dreams. Mike helped me reframe these as well. For example, he told me that it was a good thing that I had dreamed about giving my father CPR. He wanted me to look at my dream positively and see it as my way of reconnecting with my dad and doing everything I could to save him.

I could see his point, but I still dreaded having nightmares. To help me sleep, Mike asked me to bring my mind to a place of positivity and happiness or concentrate on an enjoyable memory before bed each night. He told me to hold onto these moments as I fell asleep. We have tried various techniques to help me overcome my trauma and reorient my dreams. He helped me to be patient, to give my brain, soul, and emotions time to heal as well as my body had.

My journey with Mike is still ongoing. We catch up every six to eight weeks and discuss all things living, including the latest Netflix shows. Therapy has brought a new calmness to my mind. I grieved meaningfully. I sleep better now. As days turned into weeks, months, and eventually years, I managed to navigate many stressful and anxiety-inducing life situations with Mike's help as I transitioned into new avenues and experiences. I would face more health challenges later in life and needed his guidance.

Mike has encouraged me to work less and focus more on living: "Deepak, you have climbed the mountain. It's time to start the trek back down from the top." He advised me against performing complex procedures in the Cath lab and to give up situations that induce anxiety or stress. I love performing procedures in the Cath lab, but this may be a sacrifice I must make soon to benefit my mental health. He also encouraged me to give up my administrative duties and focus on working enjoyably. He wanted me to explore more hobbies and passions.

"Deepak, it's time for self-care and self-love," he said gently. "You've spent all your life loving others and caring for others, but it is time for you to love yourself."

Mike constantly asked about how Deepa and Soorya were doing. He warned me about vicarious trauma. This is a "shared trauma" when trauma affects close family members or caregivers. No one is immune from these emotional processes. These complex situations are terrible and add to the wholesome misery of dealing with cancer. Serious and often long-lasting relationship issues arise from unresolved shared trauma, which can sometimes cause negative family dynamics. To complicate matters, vicarious trauma in cancer treatment is still poorly studied and explored. This form of trauma also greatly affects clinicians after being exposed to multiple sad and traumatic situations at work.

During our sessions, Mike introduced me to the term "Post-Cancer Stress Disorder" (PCSD). I hope this concept gains broader acceptance in the cancer community and that treating and preventing it becomes a standard part of cancer treatment.

Meeting Andrew

Friday, November 5, 2021, Zachary, Louisiana

Delta Flight 2125 departed Newark, New Jersey, on time at 8:30 a.m. Andrew texted me just before takeoff to let me know that he had made it on time. There were no major traffic issues on that chilly morning in New Jersey. He had boarded and would have a connecting flight in Atlanta to take him to Baton Rouge. We planned to meet him at the local airport around noon.

It had been nearly a year and a half since we first spoke to Andrew in July 2020, and we had all been eagerly anticipating the day we would finally meet face-to-face. We had kept in touch, and Deepa and I regularly prayed for him since he had a dangerous job as a New Jersey police officer. After that first FaceTime meeting, Andrew was promoted to the detective position, got engaged to his girlfriend, Jenna, and moved into a new house. Hurricane Ida, which devastated southern Louisiana, caused physical damage to his home in New Jersey. His basement was flooded and needed extensive repairs. When things settled down, we invited Andrew and Jenna to visit us when their schedules allowed. Jenna couldn't get time off, but Andrew was able to arrange a weekend off.

I left work early that day and drove to the airport in Baton Rouge. Deepa had driven separately and was already waiting outside when I pulled in.

It was a pleasant day in Baton Rouge, much warmer and sunnier than the forecast for New Jersey that weekend, and Deepa and I were glad that we could offer one of our angels this beauty.

Andrew's flight was early. In fact, three planes landed within ten minutes—a lot for a small airport—filling the airport with people and commotion. We had never met Andrew in person and everyone wore masks due to the ongoing COVID-19 pandemic.

Once passengers deplane in Baton Rouge, they walk through the security checkpoint into a long, expansive lobby. This lobby leads to a short escalator down to the receiving area. Deepa waited outside due to the crowd, but could see the busy receiving area through the glass doors. I stood close to the bottom of the escalator. I studied the crowd, looking for Andrew. Many people, both young and old, were coming down the escalator. I wore my scrubs, hoping it would help him identify me. Locating a middle-aged, bald Indian doctor with a shaved head wearing maroon scrubs and a broad smile in an airport in the deep south of the country shouldn't be that difficult—that was my intention.

I waited and waited until two young men came down the escalator. The first one walked past me. The second one was Andrew. He seemed to know me immediately. He walked toward me, and I walked toward him. We embraced. Holding him tightly, I whispered, "Welcome to Louisiana, Andrew." I choked up momentarily. "Thank you for saving my life."

"Don't mention it. It was my pleasure," Andrew replied. He was all smiles, cool and composed. He was dressed casually in jeans, a T-shirt, and a light jacket. His only luggage was a small backpack.

At that moment, I was full of emotions that were complex and hard to describe. I was reflecting on the vagaries of life and the Universe that had brought together two individuals from opposite corners of a vast country. Our history couldn't be more different, our life circumstances couldn't be more contrasting, yet here we were embracing each other in the lobby of an airport in South Louisiana. I felt a deep sense of awe and profound humility, as if a mysterious hand was guiding events beyond my control and imagination. It was as if the heavens and the spirits of those who had passed before me were orchestrating this moment. My knees trembled with the sheer gravity of what I was experiencing. I felt the urge to weep, but then, just as suddenly, I was filled with joy and gratitude. I was ecstatic to finally meet Andrew in person.

Outside, Deepa witnessed the moment through the glass windows. When we walked out to join her, she had tears in her eyes. She wept as she embraced Andrew, her tears a mix of joy and gratitude for his presence during our time of despair. She hugged him tightly with heartfelt emotion.

We soon reached home and opened a bottle of champagne to celebrate our meeting. Deepa had been planning this day for months. Our only regret was that Soorya was not around to welcome Andrew. We sipped champagne and talked about the day of the transplant and what a blessing his donation was to us. He told us about his experiences with his twin sister's cancer. Our conversation continued through lunch.

That night, we had some festivities planned for Andrew. Many people were eager to meet him and hold him tight. Deepa and I wanted to introduce Andrew to the local culture, so we took him to a truly traditional Southern eatery in a small town called St. Francisville on the Mississippi River. It is a unique historical town full of plantation homes. There, he met about thirty of my closest friends and staff. They hugged him and offered their appreciation for his kindness and generosity. Andrew was the star of the night, and he handled it with charm and spontaneity. He FaceTimed the rest of his family from the restaurant, including them in the festivities. I saw Megan through FaceTime for the first time and said hi to her. He got a taste of true Louisiana Cajun and Creole cuisine. He truly embraced the change of scenery and pace of living. He spent the night with us, and the following day, we drove to New Orleans in the morning and took him to Pat O'Brien's on Bourbon Street. He ate jambalaya and shrimp po'boy as he sipped the quintessential New Orleans cocktail, the hurricane. By now, he had tasted a variety of Louisiana favorites, including gumbo, Boudin balls, crawfish étouffée, sautéed crab claws, and Louisiana oysters. At one point, Andrew gleefully repeated, "I could eat this food all day and night!"

On the Bayous, we gave him a taste of southern Louisiana's unique Cajun way of life. The speedboat tour through the crisscrossing swamps was a truly magical experience. These swamps and bayous eventually drain into the Gulf of Mexico. The sights, smells, sounds, flora, and fauna are all unique to this part of Louisiana. For Andrew, one highlight of the tour was feeding the alligators that inhabit these waterways. He thoroughly enjoyed the swamp trip, though he politely declined the offer to hold a baby alligator in his hands. By now, he was culturally a million miles away from his busy life in New Jersey as a police detective. On the drive back from the bayous, we stopped at a Daiquiri drive-thru on Highway 90 and ordered a traditional cherry limeade slurry. Louisiana law allowed you to buy alcohol, drive, and consume as long as the containers were closed, another surprise for the police detective from up north. Deepa and I dropped him off in New Orleans for the weekend. He planned to explore this unique American city for two nights before flying back to New Jersey the following Monday.

The visit was truly special for us, and we will fondly remember it forever. Andrew is and will always be a part of our family--an unexpected addition who has become a permanent member. Many miracles had happened for him to be my bone marrow donor. Some are beyond the ability of modern medicine to explain or comprehend. A portion of him flows through my veins and arteries, touching my heart with every beat until the day I die. He is, quite literally, in my heart forever. He will always reside in both of our hearts, and nothing can change that.

Red, White, and Blue

During my virtual therapy session on a Tuesday afternoon in mid-March 2023, Mike, my therapist, assumed a brief meditative posture. His eyes were partially closed, and he had a smile on his face. His room was well-lit, and a bright yellow light fell on his face as he spoke. He soon opened his eyes, and a broader smile came through. And then, he started laughing out loud in his unique way. "Deepak, I want you to pray and meditate about July 4th. It could be the last day of your work, your Independence Day."

I had finished my office work early and wanted to update Mike on the steps I was taking on my "trek down the mountain," as he once put it—an empowering image for my healing from the high stress summits of my cancer journey and its attendant PTSD. I could slowly back away from the high adrenaline clench of the past five years only by retracing the arduous steps I'd clambered to survive.

The Universe has been revealing truths I had been ignoring. I could no longer disregard my body's needs or forego attending to the even deeper healing my soul clamored for repeatedly. He knew that a change for me was essential, but he also knew that the change posed more stress and anxiety for me. Lately, this has been the predominant theme in our sessions. "Mike, I am almost done with the trek," I told him.

In reality, my spirit already departed from the mountains. My nights like hiking packs full of dreams tracing a single-file pathway through valleys, stopping only at ocean shores. In the valleys of serenity, calm prevailed. Gentle breezes tendered fresh bulbs as they secretly kissed each other. Angels became butterflies, and bees lusted for honey. Hummingbirds landed on my shoulder. I was watching life as it should be and I could stay there forever. But I yearned for something else. My mind always took the same route, aiming for the shores.

The narrow path soon led me to the ocean, and I stopped. It took my breath away. We both had to process emotions. Soon, the waves came out to me and touched my feet. They couldn't control their happiness. They kept coming and lashed onto the shores. I was their companion once upon a time—their playmate. The coconut trees saw me and swayed their heads. They had a rhythm as if they were playing in a band. Palm leaves shone, polished by the evening sun. They trembled as they took in the breeze and played a welcoming ballad for me. Soon, they refreshed their memories. I had grown old and sick, and so had they. They had slanted more to the water as if carrying the world's weight. No children were around, climbing on their backs and jumping into the stream.

The stream grew narrower and more emaciated, losing its luster. The monsoon had yet to arrive. With the rains, "my" stream would regain her fullness and beauty. By then, she would care even less about me, as she rushed to meet her ultimate lover, the ocean, as she always did, season after season.

One after another, my childhood friends arrived, followed by the fishermen. The small wooden boats had disappeared, replaced by large, motorized ones. They brought their children and grandchildren. We drank sweet toddy from clay pots, sitting together facing the ocean. The sun dipped into the sea, casting its golden rays on my face. We had a lot to catch up on, as times had changed and many moons had passed. The trauma of life was evident on their faces and mine was no different. As a cancer survivor with access to the best treatment, I felt a profound survivor's guilt, knowing that many of my friends had not been as fortunate.

I listened to their sorrows and how the rain washed them away. They lived and died by the shore; their lives became stories, no different from what will be mine, soon to be forgotten. The stream, perpetually in motion, carried these sorrows into the ocean. Many mango trees were cut, and clay pots were thrown into the sea. These pots were covered in beautiful red silk with yellow borders and adorned with wildflowers from the family compounds. Priests chanted prayers and led the grieving people to the ocean like a procession. The sea was waiting for the souls' arrival—the homecoming. The skeletal remains washed up on the shore, accompanied by wildflowers.

The free and liberated souls then stayed around the shore. Some chose to be shooting stars. Just like their life on earth, they were all gone in a blink. The freed souls by the shore watched the living and waited. The sea, too, waited patiently.

I continued to ponder about the long-gone years. The breeze comforted me and wiped my tears. Soon, it was dark, and I was ready to sleep. The friends and fishermen had all gone to their homes, and the children waved their goodbyes. The golden sand became my bed once again, and I found myself sleeping rough on the same cancerous sand. The moon emerged from behind the clouds, casting its light on the empty land. There was no noise except for the ocean trying to tell me things. Those murmurs from the waves soothed my soul as I stared at the sky and talked to the friends I had lost. One by one, they appeared as shooting stars. I apologized for not being there for them, caught up in life in distant and unfamiliar lands, leading a fast life, not knowing what I was truly after. What was I searching for that was worth leaving these shores? Would I have caught cancer if I had never left these shores? I had no answers as I gazed at the star-filled horizon. But now, I am a free man. I realized I no longer needed to wake up early, like in my high school years, to avoid being caught by my parents. I could sleep until the sun was up.

At work, the feeling of leaving the mountains behind me was getting more comfortable and less anxiety-provoking. It is out in the open now. I had been talking to and preparing my staff and team at the office and hospital. For many, I was the only boss they had ever known, and they needed time to get used to my absence and move forward without me. I assured them that my partners would take good care of them.

I also informed my patients about my departure from the practice. They hated the notion and instantly assumed that I was sick again. "Is the cancer back?" They all asked, worry and care inscribing their faces. I reassured them that the cancer had not returned. Many of them teared up upon learning of my departure. They hugged me and wished me the best. They all wanted me to keep in touch. I ensured they were matched with doctors who suited their specific problems and personalities. My goal was to leave the practice in peace, knowing they were all well taken care of, fulfilling my commitment to my beloved patients. My patients had always placed me on a pedestal I felt I did not deserve.

Mike couldn't be happier. He only suggested that I choose July 4th as the last day of work, freeing myself from the shackles of back-breaking American work life.

My last day at work marked the end of a journey that took me from a coastal village in South India to three continents and two major international cities. This work brought me immense pleasure and satisfaction as I saved countless lives and mentored numerous professionals. I taught kindness and compassion and demonstrated the profound healing power of touch and hugs. There is nothing more magical than the healing power of touch; it remains the most potent remedy.

Serving the community of Zachary and nearby counties has been a blessing. Establishing a cardiology program that the community can be proud of has been a special privilege, playing a crucial role in saving countless lives. We stayed far away from the deep-pocketed interests of industry and focused on science and merit. Our small community-based program has served as a road map for many programs in the state. Ours is a program built on kindness, where only kind people work. We are known for our compassion and the genuine care we provide.

My work as a busy procedure specialist has saved countless lives. It has also caused unintentional consequences and harm. It is meant to happen to all of us in this field. You are in God's territory when you work on a beating heart. There are no minor complications when it comes to the heart. The same was true with my work on the arteries to the brain. The brain is unforgiving. One could lose a precious life in front of your eyes. It has happened to me. It is destined to happen to all of us in this field. Our work takes us to the boundaries separating life and death in the middle of the day or night. These boundaries remain fluid yet palpable. As a specialist, it is also true that I can bring a dying heart to its full glory. Seeing these folks walk out of the hospital with their families is fantastic. Heart attacks and cardiac arrests have no calendar invitations, nor do they take any holidays. When you are an interventional cardiologist, the God of death, Yama Raj, hides in your shadow. The great Lord Vishnu, the preserver of all things living, almost always prevails over Yama Raj. Hence, almost always, life triumphs over death. This truth fuels our souls and keeps us moving forward.

My work involved working with radiation for long hours, possibly contributing to my cancer. But I consciously avoided looking back to chastise myself. Yes, there were instances where I wished I had been more careful with radiation. But that was the past, and I am moving forward.

Mike recommended a "tune-up." Focus on finding a "body shop" of sorts, one that revolved around the mind-body-soul axis. My own chassis, warped and rusted with the long-term side effects of stem cell transplant, needed thorough care. My immune system was still in the process of recovery. I was not fully vaccinated yet, which has prevented me from traveling to India to visit my eighty-six-year-old mother. She missed me terribly. Mike prompted me to pray for optimum immune counts. "It works like magic," he told me. Ah, I thought. My old friend, targeted meditation, which every healer in my life taught me. "A trip to the homeland would complete a circle of life and healing for you," Mike continued. "Immerse yourself in the ancient healing techniques of yoga, ayurveda, and meditation."

He drew an imaginary circle in the air for me and finished the session by gently and kindly waving to me.

Circle of Life and Healing

July 4, 2023. My last day of work in Louisiana.

I had wound up my clinical responsibilities. We recruited a new cardiologist from Staten Island, New York, earlier that year, and I'd stayed at work for a few more months until he was comfortable and the patients got used to him. Newly minted cardiologists, fresh out of training, were often overconfident, but were humbled quickly.

For us seasoned professionals, all too familiar. We were them once, a finger's snap of time ago that was in reality, decades of learning from our mistakes and learning to be vulnerable enough to collaborate with others. To listen more and more deeply to our own patients and to our intuition stripped of arrogance.

In the last week of June, David organized a well-attended send-off party. He gave an eloquent and emotional speech, choking up as he described my journey, from the day he first met me in a dimly lit room at the famed Sparks Steak House on the east side of Manhattan in late 2007. He had traveled to meet me with Joey Fontenot, then the Chief Operating Officer for the company. Our friendship had grown ever since as the families grew closer. He had commissioned a famous sculptor from Austin to create a bronze sculpture representing my craft. It was simply stunning and weighed a ton. The city of Zachary sent an official who read a proclamation on my behalf. I prepared a speech, which I managed to complete. We hugged and said our goodbyes. That day marked the end of my story in Zachary, though our friendships and our dear memories will echo forever.

Deepa and I packed our bags the following day and drove west through Louisiana, Texas, and New Mexico. We wished to take Soorya along on this trip, but he couldn't get time off from the military. He has been enjoying his time with the Air Force and was deployed overseas in the dunes of Saudi Arabia and the Qatari desert. While in Saudi Arabia, he received many accolades, including recognition as the best airman of Centcom, which represents the deployed forces of the United States military. He would go on to get many more awards while at Andrews Air Force Base in Washington, DC, where he was stationed (Yes, Andrew my donor and Andrews twinned in my family's story!). Most importantly, he has forged countless friendships within the Air Force and has had the opportunity to serve this great nation with pride and honor.

Deepa did most of the driving. The landscape passing by reminded us of the long and varied routes our lives had taken in our working life together.

We had not planned much for this vacation to celebrate my retirement except for the destination: the Colorado Rockies.

As we grew tired, we booked rooms in nearby hotels along the highway. After two days of driving, we arrived in Estes Park, Colorado, following a brief stay in Colorado Springs.

As we arrived at Estes Park, Andrew messaged to inform us that his twin Megan had passed away. Her body rejected her heart transplant, the very definition of heart-breaking. We knew she had been struggling, but it was a shock. We felt deeply for Andrew and his family. Although we had only met Megan once, at Andrew's wedding, we felt very close to her. Deepa had brought a small, hand-made Ganapati statue, which we presented to Megan when we met her. She was ever so thankful and appreciated the gift. Although there were no words to comfort Andrew, I left a voice message on his phone.

In the remaining months of the summer, I had to deal with more health issues and underwent two hip surgeries.

I was delaying these surgeries for fear of complications. I had bad hips for a long time, the origins of which happened when we were in middle school. This resulted in a slight disparity in the lengths of my legs and subsequently led to arthritis, which was obviously worsened by the intense chemotherapy and high doses of steroids I had to take for months to treat the GVHD. I was delaying the surgery because of the fear of non-healing or infection, due to my low immune counts.

However, by July 2023, I had decided to proceed with the surgery, and on the 20th, I underwent the first surgery, followed by rehabilitation. During the follow-up visit, I was told about the rare complication of a spontaneous fracture of a piece of the femoral head and the need to go back and proceed with a rather extensive surgery, removing the previously placed hardware. The re-do surgery was in the first week of September, which led to significant blood loss.

I came out of the surgery with my left leg looking like it was run over by a train. My spirit was crushed again. My mind played tricks after surgery, and there was a resurgence of anxiety, though I was able to control it with deep breathing and meditation.

Mike was worried too, and he kept in touch with me. I discussed my symptoms with him, which were all too familiar to him. He recommended that I ask for medications to alleviate anxiety. Fortunately, I did not need any help with those medications. I went back to true self meditation and was able to keep my anxiety at bay. Deepa was worried again after the second surgery and the blood loss. After the second surgery, we stayed back in Houston for two more weeks to be careful. I was not allowed full weight bearing for the next six weeks. The fatigue and pain were real. I was back using a walker, which then graduated to a cane. Soon, I was cleared for rehab after the follow-up visit. The grueling rehab went on through December of that year.

While I was undergoing rehab, Deepa was busy packing up our Louisiana home. I felt bad that I was in no position to help. But we were both excited for a move back to Brooklyn.

On December 12th, a Tuesday, the movers left for a two-day trip to New York, carrying our household items. Once they left, I knelt on the nicely trimmed grass next to my garage and kissed the ground—my goodbye to a land that had adopted me as a son. It was here that I faced profound tests and felt the boundless love of the land and its people. The love had no boundaries, and I experienced unending love from Louisiana and the black and white people of this state.

I also wanted to leave this chapter of sickness and difficulties behind me, having endured more suffering than one might in a lifetime.

I hoped for a fresh start, filled with health and well-being. Deepa prayed for a new, healthy beginning in New York. Adding to that was the excitement of being close to our only son. Washington, DC, was a few hours' drive away, finally making it possible for us to be a family again.

On the second night of our drive to the Big Apple, we stopped in North Carolina, a small town outside Durham, and stayed with friends, who lavished us with a home-cooked Kerala meal. From there, we drove to our furnished apartment in Brooklyn. Just across the water our possessions from our Baton Rouge home were stored.

Before we even had a chance to set up our new home, we flew to India to complete the circle of healing. This time, my worries about my immune status and the risk of international travel took a back seat. It had been far too long. Seven years. And a miracle to be going back.

Our Qatar Airways flight took off from JFK to Doha on January 2, 2024. I had mistakenly booked the morning flight out of JFK airport instead of an evening departure, which resulted in a rather long layover in Doha. Deepa wasn't happy. It took fifteen hours to reach Doha. The connecting flight landed at Calicut International Airport on January 4th at 2:00 a.m. I hadn't been able to sleep on the plane.

We cleared security and the customs checkpoint and walked out through the exit. Our driver, who had driven from Kannur the evening before and camped out at the airport, was waiting for us in the early morning hours. As was a light drizzle buffeted by a gentle breeze—the first rain of the season. The airport was unusually quiet, just a few scattered taxi drivers. In the dim parking lot, I searched for an empty piece of non-paved land. I glimpsed a patch of grass next to the taxi stand with rose bushes dotted with roses.

I walked as steadily as I could after such a long flight and all the years it had taken me to return to my homeland. Standing still for a moment in the dry grass, I gazed at the empty sky and thanked the gods and the Universe for this moment of return. The Universe had cradled me like a baby when I needed it most.

Needing to get closer, I sat on the grass, touched the sand, and gently kissed the ground. Almost not making it sent chills down my spine. So many events, some beyond the realm of our understanding, had led to me kneeling on the ground outside an international airport in northern Kerala in the middle of the night, under a light January drizzle. Another transformation.

I quietly got back into the car. Deepa had witnessed the moment in awe and surprise. She had tears in her eyes as she held me tightly.

The drive took about three hours. Rain condensed into a scrim over the windshield and thunder and lightning did their song and dance above us, a celestial welcome.

Midway through the trip, as we passed the old French colony of Mahé, we stopped for refreshments at a *thattu kada*, a makeshift tea stall by the highway, common and cherished by nighttime travelers.

Pulling into Kannur, it was still dark. We were staying in an apartment complex perched on a cliff. The unit was on the 13th floor, which granted us panoramic views of the Arabian Sea. I had purchased this apartment many years ago but had never had the opportunity to stay there until now. It was the perfect setting for my homecoming, allowing me to feel close to the ocean every moment of my waking hours. The sea breeze was constant, sometimes intensifying to howling winds. Like life.

A walkway from the apartment building led to the beach through a park with plenty of trees and ample shade. This long stretch of land by the sea has golden sand adorned with stately coconut trees. Many dignitaries of the state of Kerala were laid to rest on this beach, and monuments were erected on their behalf. Every morning, I saw funeral processions walk from the funeral home to the ocean, only a few feet away. They all carried ceremonial clay pots and were accompanied by priests. It was here that Deepa's father was cremated, Soorya carrying his ashes to the ocean.

My time in Kerala was blissful. I felt a profound freedom from the clutches of work. I had time to process my emotions and felt deeply connected to Kerala's pristine beaches and the sea, which had always been my first love. The people on these shores are etched into my soul forever. The many tragedies I witnessed have shaped me, and our customs, steeped in history, have a way of grounding me. The clay pots that carried our souls to the Universe, the mango tree ritual, and the act of liberating the soul into the ocean symbolize the completion of the circle of life in a deeply earthy manner. The sea, where life began as we know it, remains a powerful reminder of our origins.

Each day, I walked to the ocean and let the crashing waves tender my sickly body for hours at a time. The seawater and the salt nurtured and healed my skin. I lay on the beach in the shade, listening to the waves and the ocean. I made friends with street dogs feeding them in the mornings. One dog, whom I named Rani, took a particular liking to me. She followed me daily to the water and babysat my clothes and phone as I dipped in the sea. The ocean was gentle with no dangerous waves, though I was careful not to be pulled into the rip currents.

I had never truly left those shores.

Eight weeks passed like a breeze. We celebrated my mother's eighty-seventh birthday all together. She was a bit frail, but could still navigate the house without assistance, though she carried a wooden stick for safety. Clear-minded and intelligent as always, she managed her finances independently. The home nurse cooked meals for her.

I sat by the ground where my father's and grandmother's funeral pyres were lit. I thanked them for staying with me during my difficult journey. I often felt their presence, not to mention my feelings about my grandmother's role in having a common ancestry with Andrew.

Deepa and I stayed in the same upstairs room where I had grown up. Prior to our arrival, my eldest sister had cleared the cobwebs and the

too-comfortable spiders and hired a painter to refresh the walls. Luckily, the air conditioning unit was still functional, though it was a bit tem-
peramental. Kerala is starved of electricity like many Asian countries,
and power cuts are frequent.

I also attended a few more family gatherings, reconnecting with
many cousins, nieces, and nephews.

This trip allowed me to immerse myself in the various healing
pathways that India offers, and there were many. One has to be open to
possibilities outside the realm of modern medicine and science. I believe
in science and have a deep understanding of it, having practiced as a
physician for many years across three continents. However, I also recognize the value of exploring alternative healing methods. I have attained
a mark of Distinction in examinations from Mangalore University and
the University of London. I hold the coveted Fellowship of the Royal
Colleges in the United Kingdom and the American College of Cardiology. I have reached the pinnacle of academic success as an Interventional
Cardiologist and have seven board certifications under my name, a rarity
in the United States.

Yet, through my cancer treatment, I have understood the limits to
and the deficiencies in our current medical knowledge. I had to choose a
less-trodden path. I considered myself someone with a strong mind, yet
cancer broke my spirit and cast a long shadow of self-doubt, angst, and
sadness. PTSD is real in the cancer world, and the medical community
is woefully inadequate in treating this mental damage from cancer. This
cancer of the mind plays games with you, and I realized that it is okay
to feel lonely and vulnerable. It is okay to be sad and depressed. But
know that for complete health, we must strive not to ignore feelings of
despondency. Staying human comes with a price in these modern times,
and probably always has.

I checked into the practice of a well-known Ayurvedic physician
in Kannur soon after my arrival there. Kerala has a deep tradition of
Ayurvedic medicine. No chemicals or artificial agents are involved in
producing Ayurvedic medicines, only roots, herbs, and the like. It also
involves special massage techniques with medicated oils and yoga. This

treatment was based on ancient wisdom rooted in centuries of practice. The physician was concerned that my blood was "hot" and wanted to cool it, while also focusing on removing toxins from my system. He prescribed ayurvedic medicines, which I consumed multiple times daily. He also prescribed a special herbal oil, which I applied while sitting on my apartment balcony to expose myself to the sun. There was strict dieting, and only vegetarian food was allowed while on treatment. This treatment went on for six weeks while I was in Kannur. The physician had graciously arranged for the medicines to be taken back to the United States, along with duly filled-out customs forms, as there are restrictions in some countries regarding the import of Ayurvedic medicines.

Choosing the road less traveled, exploring the possibilities of self-healing, and finding the cure is perfectly acceptable. Ayurveda is one of the lesser-known modalities of medicine in the Western world. These doctors go through Ayurvedic medical schools and understand how the body and mind are connected. They also understand how the universe works in different ways to modulate human functions. Their training lasted five years, similar to a medical degree program, and upon completion, they were awarded an MD degree in Ayurveda.

Understanding our origins can accelerate healing and is liberating. Separating the soul from the mind helps ease the pain and misery associated with cancer and its treatment. Sitting and pondering by the sea into the evening hours gave me clarity. I realized that today, I am closer to the Universe than ever before. The cancer that took root in me and my acquaintance with mortality made me realize this closeness. I also learned that all living and nonliving things arise from the Universe's eternal energy source—indestructible, yet soothing and compassionate.

While at Kannur, I trained under a guruji in deep breathing exercises and breathing-aided meditation. These sessions lasted for hours during the day; most sessions were group sessions where one could interact with fellow trainees. At the end of each session, my heart was full of gratitude that I had been given a second chance to enjoy the ancient and traditional Indian ways of healing and curing one's body and mind. This breathing-mediated meditation involved repeating alternate slow and fast breathing. The guruji carried himself lightly and with humor, which cast the questions he asked me with particular poignancy. "Dear son, how long do you plan to stay in this world?" followed by "Son, what is your purpose in this life?"

I struggled to answer the guruji truthfully and fully. He offered himself as a stand-in for myself, a conduit. Existential questions usually require a deep, often uncomfortable toggling to find answers. Guruji advised against rushing the process. He said the answers would come to me gradually, becoming clear as daylight at the right time. He insisted that I focus on living in the present and avoid unnecessary worry about the future. "Live in the present and greet each day with gratitude."

Sessions with the holy man reinforced my feelings about the greatness and vastness of the Universe. Our souls are a manifestation of the Universe. They are a source of constant energy, fueling our contentment and happiness. They are the origin of spirituality within us and the divinity we seek. Our experiences in the orchestra of life format and structure the mind. Whichever instrument you play in this orchestra will undoubtedly lead to despair, insecurity, anger, immense happiness, and joy. Learning to accept happiness and despair equally is like living with the changing seasons. One must learn to tolerate happiness and distress equally without being disturbed by them, just as we must learn to accept the chills of winter and the heat of summer.

Along with the guidance of guruji I invariably went into a trance and slept unknowingly, as my mind and body were calm and relaxed during sessions. Guruji recommended that I do these sessions every day. These could last up to 25 minutes daily, preferably in the morning.

I planned to visit the Ganges and meditate by its shore during this trip. However, Deepa was not keen on the idea. She feared I would catch a sickness in big crowds, which is usually true in holy cities like Varanasi by the Ganges. I listened to her and abstained.

As days went by, my lungs felt better, and I could breathe more deeply despite having transplantation-induced lung damage. My joints felt looser, and my surgical scars healed. My skin tone improved as my pores sweated profusely during the day and night amidst the intense humidity of Kerala. The saltwater from the ocean cleansed me with its minerals and washed away my sorrows.

Soon, it was time to return.

Back on QR 537 in Doha on March 12, 2024, and from there, after a brief stopover, to JFK on the same day. I stayed awake for most of the trip, planning my future, now that I felt more confident that I had one. I felt with a deep certainty that I had not yet played out all the acts in the drama that was my life.

What is the purpose for the remainder of my life, and how long do I plan to stay in the Universe?

I felt drawn to teaching on a part-time basis, where I could reinforce the core concepts of kindness and empathy to the new generation of doctors. I had already reached out to my old program in Brooklyn and the Chairman for a part-time opportunity.

Of course, I am just another blood count away from a relapse. Should the worst happen, I am more prepared for it now. I know the part required of me, having played it before. The first act was hard; I may not perform it again. But as the years pass, I think less and less of this possibility. Instead, I have a newfound eagerness for life and all it offers. I have finished the trek down the mountain of my professional life and hope to explore new pastures. I knew that I wanted to be of service, though I am still discovering what that means. I am also filled with gratitude. It is the predominant feeling I have throughout my waking hours.

Deepa and I often reflected on our journey as a couple, amazed by the decisions we had made over the years. We reminisced about the journeys we had taken and the oceans we had crossed. We had faced real and challenging struggles together as a family. Ours was an American immigrant story, and like many immigrants, we started our journey in New York. We are ever so grateful to be in this country. The heart of America is pure, unadulterated kindness. An immeasurable expanse of love so vast and deep as the Universe itself. It defies the definition of a sacred place in the world one could call home. It is an emotion, an idea, an endless and unbound spirit that brings prosperity and stability to the broader world. I am so glad that my son joined the United States Air Force to protect the very ideals of this nation. Ever so proud as a father.

We also wondered about our fate, which had brought us to this country and eventually to Louisiana. Was it all by chance? Whether through fate or pure chance, I happened to be living close to the best cancer center in the world. The best chance to save my life was an afternoon's drive away.

While stumbling through the labyrinthine hallways of MD Anderson, my road diverged from others' paths. As in most of life, we can't always tell which way we're headed, but we can, to some extent, guide our journey. It's important to remember this and to persevere, to delve deep into oneself if, Dear Reader, cancer pays an unannounced visit. My journey bears that out.

Our one human certainty is that a day will come when we return to the arms of the Universe. I will have chosen my tree and experienced long arborous conversations just like my grandmother did. My son will then free my soul in clay pots covered in silk and adorned with beautiful fresh flowers, sending it to the waiting ocean, my wife standing behind him in knee-deep waters, her legs caressed by the waves, soothing her spirits.

I will be happy at home—final homecoming.

Postscript: Words From My Son

It's been a long road. One of the doctors from the very beginning said that this would be a marathon, not a sprint. Looking back, that feels more accurate than I could have imagined as we reflect on everything that happened to us—and everything we did in response.

I still remember being out that day when I got the call. It was the kind of news I couldn't fully process, so I went home and contemplated what it all meant. To make matters worse, I only had part of the story. I was painting an incomplete picture in my mind, and the wait to fill it in meant more time spent with all manner of thoughts swirling around my head. Slowly, the information trickled in, and I began to grasp the magnitude of what we were dealing with.

Luckily, my education equipped me to understand the theory behind this cancer and some of what the treatment would entail, so I began researching and found enough to be cautiously optimistic. There was so much about those first few days that was a blur, but one moment still stands out.

It was during the initial consult when the doctors started articulating the short-term plan. My dad spoke at length with the team lead and assured them that he was in full support of whatever they thought was best. He ended the conversation with, "I'm in your hands."

I don't think it was just the words—it was the way he said them:

cheerfully and confidently. It felt like he wasn't merely reminding the doctors to do their best, but that he already knew they were doing their best. He had boundless confidence in their abilities and in their character, and he wanted them to know that. I was proud of that.

That moment—and many more—have shaped our family in ways we both do and do not understand. Moments where I saw a side of humanity I never thought I would: one that embodied resilience and grace, qualities I had mostly encountered through the epic tales of fiction I've enjoyed throughout my life—stories that celebrated the indomitable human spirit.

Moments where I saw my parents stretched to the breaking point and return to hope. Moments where I started asking questions of myself and the universe I never imagined I would. Moments where I saw the already extraordinary generosity of our friends reach new heights. Moments where I saw a community rally in ways I had only ever seen from the outside. Moments where I saw an institution operate in ways that gave me hope for institutions everywhere. Moments where I witnessed the miracles of science take effect in profound and spectacular ways. Moments where relationships formed from a shared experience and still stand firm to this day. Moments that made this book—and so much more—possible.

There's so much more I could say, but my dad says it all and more.

—**Soorya**

A Letter From My Donor

Growing up, I always understood what it meant to fight, even if I wasn't the one fighting. I am a twin. My sister Megan and I came into this world together a few minutes apart. She was then diagnosed with leukemia as an infant, and I've heard the stories of her early battles. Although I was too young to remember those first days, I've always felt like they shaped something in me. People often say twins share a special bond, and I believe that. Even as a baby, I think I felt her absence when she was sick. Her fight didn't end after beating leukemia, she had a stroke and later received a heart transplant. Through every hospital visit, scary moment, and text message, I was there. Not just to be present but to make her laugh. That was my job—to keep her smiling. From the early days, I developed an instinct to protect her and keep her happy.

There were countless times I wished I could have done more. Watching someone you love fight for their life repeatedly leaves a mark on your soul. I saw how much small moments meant to her: a text from a friend, a surprise visit from family, the therapy dog stopping by her room, and, of course, the incredible care from the doctors and nurses. These things mattered. They reminded her, and all of us, that people cared. That she wasn't fighting alone. What she doesn't know is how much she has shaped me. The way she lived her life, with resilience, humor, and heart, taught me what strength looks like, and that's the reason I became a police officer.

Every day, I put on a vest to save and protect others, a role I've always felt drawn to. This same motivation led me to seek another way to help—which is how I found Be The Match.

I signed up for the registry because it felt like the right thing to do. It was 2013, during a Relay for Life event for my twin. The process was surprisingly simple: I swabbed, sent it in, and then forgot about the registry until I received a life-changing call.

I was at work, sitting in patrol car 22, which just happens to be my lucky number. My phone kept ringing with an unknown caller. I ignored it at first. Seconds later, the same number called again, and something told me to answer. The female operator introduced herself and asked if I remembered swabbing for a match. I said, "Yes." She then told me I was a match and asked if I was still willing to donate. I responded immediately, "Yes, I would love to." I didn't think twice.

Once the dates and times were set, I was treated exceptionally well. They sent a nurse to my house to begin the preparation process. My command staff arranged everything and granted me the time off. On the day of the donation, the registry sent a limousine to pick me up. I remember sitting in the donation chair, hooked up and ready, and sending a picture to my family. My sister was the first to respond, telling me how proud she was.

Throughout the process, I got subtle hints that my recipient had a family and was far away from me. After the donation, a volunteer came in and collected the marrow, and I found out he was catching a plane immediately to head south. I was told it would be a five-hour trip. The entire experience was smooth, well-organized, and I felt constantly supported and reassured by the medical team and my family.

Donating was another way for me to protect someone and give a stranger a chance to live life to the fullest, just as my sister was given through her heart transplant. What I didn't expect was the profound impact this donation would have on me. Over time, I got to know Deepak and his family. We went from being strangers to becoming a family. I visited Deepa and Deepak in Louisiana. Soorya came to visit us and stayed with us. They came to my wedding, met my family, and most importantly, Megan, before she passed. Now we are bonded in a way that's hard to put into words; it's more than just a medical connection, rather a human and lifelong one. It all started with a simple decision to join someone's fight.

If I could do it all over again, I wouldn't hesitate.

—**Andrew**

Silk and Clay

Acknowledgments

My journey wouldn't have been possible without the endless love and care of my wife and our son. They are my rocks, the ones I lean on when I am weak or struggling. I am deeply grateful to my mother and the rest of my family—my siblings, friends, coworkers, patients, the clergy, and the community in and around Zachary and Baton Rouge, Louisiana — who prayed for me and held prayer meetings on my behalf. Donna, you are an angel among us, and we don't have enough words to express our love for the kindness and empathy you and Chuck have shown us during our time of need. I am especially thankful to Dr. Caring for her thoughtful and soulful approach to healing, as well as to the other doctors, nurses, and paramedical staff at MD Anderson Cancer Center and every other hospital and clinic where I received care. I appreciate David and the rest of my practice crew who stood beside me during my illness. I am forever grateful to Mike, my therapist, for his ongoing thoughtful and compassionate guidance. I wish to express my sincere gratitude to my publishing team who has guided me through the process: Phuc Luu; my editor, Jessica Cole; Kate Martin Williams of Bloomsday Literary; and photographer Paula Nguyen Luu. Additionally, I am thankful for Elisabeth Chretien, who helped during the initial stages as a developmental editor, and Shoba Rajeev from Kerala, who did a great job with line editing.

I extend my heartfelt thanks to Andrew and his family for their kindness, generosity, and the gift of life—may his tribe increase.

Lastly, I thank the Universe for the gift of my life.

About the Author

Dr. Deepak Thekkoott is a Brooklyn-based cardiologist known for combining clinical excellence with compassionate care. With decades of international experience in the U.S. and U.K., he currently practices at Maimonides Medical Center and helps train the next generation of heart specialists. A fellow of both the American College of Cardiology and the Royal College of Physicians, he holds seven board certifications in cardiovascular medicine. Born and educated in southern India, Dr. Thekkoott brings a global perspective to his work and life. He lives in Brooklyn with his wife, Deepa, and finds joy in serving others with what he calls "a heart filled with love." His son, Soorya, is pursuing graduate studies in mathematics after completing active duty service with the Washington, DC Air National Guard.